# K100 Course Team

## Original production team

Andrew Northedge (Chair)
Jan Walmsley (Deputy Chair)
Margaret Allott (Course Manager)
Tanya Hames (Course Secretary)
Joanna Bornat
Hilary Brown
Celia Davies
Roger Gomm
Sheila Peace
Martin Robb
Deborah Cooper (VQ Centre)

Jill Alger, Julie Fletcher (Editors); Janis Gilbert (Graphic Artist);
Hannah Brunt, Rob Williams (Designers); Paul Smith (Librarian);
Deborah Bywater (Project Control Assistant); Ann Carter (Print
Buying Controller); Pam Berry (Text Processing Services); Mike Levers
(Photographer); Vic Lockwood, Alison Tucker, Kathy Wilson
(BBC Producers); Maggie Guillon (Cartoonist)

## Regional Education and Training Managers

Lindsay Brigham
Anne Fletcher
Carole Ulanowsky

## External assessor

Professor Lesley Doyal, University of Bristol

This is the K100 core course team. Many other people also contributed
to making the course and their names are given in the Introduction and
Study Guide.

## Revision team

Andrew Northedge (Chair)
Corinne Pennifold (Course Manager)
Christine Wild (Course Team Assistant)
James Blewett
Joanna Bornat
Hilary Brown
Sue Cusworth
Celia Davies
Marion Dunlop
Pam Foley
Tom Heller
Vijay Patel
Sheila Peace
Lucy Rai
Marion Reichart
Angela Russell
Geraldine Lee-Treweek
Danielle Turney
Jan Walmsley
Jo Warner

Hannah Brunt (Designer); Deborah Bywater (Project Control); Maggie Gullion (Cartoonist); Sarah Hack (Graphic Artist); Lucy Hendy (Compositor); Julie Fletcher and Denise Lulham (Editors)

## Critical readers

Fiona Harkes, Sylvia Caveney, Gillian Thompson, Katy Sainsbury, Eunice Lumsden, Lynne Fisher, Margaret Brown, Paula Faller, Kate Stilliard.

## External reviewers

Professor Gordon Grant, University of Sheffield; Mary McColgan, University of Ulster; Nigel Porter, University of Portsmouth

## External assessor

Professor Gordon Grant, University of Sheffield

# Contents

Study skills by Andrew Northedge

# Introduction

In this final block of the course we are going to step back from the daily business of care to consider policy at national level. Are there plans for care in the way that there are policies for education, for social security or for economic development? Or do politicians and policy makers turn a blind eye and hope that caring will be 'kept in the family'? Do governments think about matters such as education and training for care as a whole – or have they allowed developments to occur in ways that are more of a patchwork than a pattern – to use the words in the title of Unit 26? Answers to questions about national policy sometimes seem a long way removed from the front line of care – but policies provide a framework and shape the quality of care that can be given.

There are just three units in this last block. Unit 26 takes a topic that has been a thread running through many previous units – namely, the skills that are needed to carry out caring work – and it explores the education and training that is currently available for people who wish to work in this field. It considers vocational qualifications and professional qualifications and the way the line has been drawn between the two. Unit 27 takes a historical look at how policy and provision has evolved. It explores how some of the underlying ideas have changed over time as well as starting to speculate on the future. Both units provide you with new material in the familiar way. You will find, however, that they also encourage you to look back at previous blocks and start drawing the various threads together. Unit 28 takes this further. It deliberately contains very little that is new and is designed to help you along the road to revision. By the time you have finished Block 7, the whole course will be coming together in your mind and you will be ready for that final surge of revision before the exam.

# Unit 26

# Qualifications in Caring: Pattern or Patchwork?

Prepared for the course team by Celia Davies

Updated by Celia Davies with advice from Sue Cusworth and Marion Dunlop

---

While you are working on Unit 26, you will need:

- Course Reader
- Offprints Book
- *The Good Study Guide*
- Audio Cassette 7, side 1
- *Getting a Vocational Qualification: A K100 Student's Guide*
- Wallchart

# Contents

# Introduction

We have seen throughout the course that many people find themselves doing care work at some point in their lives. Some choose it at an early stage. They prepare by taking courses and gaining qualifications and can see a career mapped out before them. Others come into care in a less planned way. They may have shorter and sometimes on-the-job training. Yet others, particularly those who find themselves doing caring work on an unpaid basis for family or friends, will have no formal preparation at all.

We can think of all these very different kinds of people as *the total workforce carrying out health and social care*. This workforce is very large. It ranges all the way from that family member (often, but not always, a daughter staying at home to care for a dependent parent) to the social worker and the highly paid hospital consultant. There are decisions to be taken for this workforce about:

- the different levels of skill that care work needs
- the types of basic training that should be available
- the further learning and development that are required
- the rewards and respect that are due to those who do care work.

These are the main issues to be considered in this unit and we will explore them by focusing on the following core questions.

---

**Core questions**

- Who can be counted as part of the care sector workforce?
- What are the problems involved in defining care skills?
- Does a distinction between professionally and vocationally trained staff make sense?
- Is there a coherent training framework that provides opportunities for progression for staff at all levels, and enhances the quality of care services?

---

# Section 1

# Who's who in health and social care?

To answer this question we would ideally start by taking a snapshot of all the different care sector workers together and asking how many different jobs there are and how many people work in each of them. In practice, this is particularly difficult to do. The answers are not readily available. Let us see what we can gather together first about the paid workforce and then about the unpaid one.

## 1.1   Piecing together the paid workforce

| Activity 1 | Reviewing care occupations |
|---|---|
| *Allow about 10 minutes* | Spend a little time writing down as many job titles as you can think of which describe people who work in health and social care. Think about your own experience. Think about different care settings. Also, glance back at some of the earlier units, especially those in Blocks 1 and 2, to lengthen your list. |

| Comment | One of the easiest ways to begin making a list is to consider a care setting: the GP surgery, the day centre or residential home, for example. Just thinking about care workers in a hospital should take your list into double figures, and a glance at the first two blocks, adding in childminders, care managers, home carers, key workers and so on, is likely to bring it up to more than 20 job titles that are about direct care. This is before you even consider clerical, managerial and other support staff who also work in the care sector. |

**H1**

**29 April**

# count me in
### Census2001

**England Household Form**

Name

Address

Postcode

CD

ED

Form Number

* Form **1** of

*Multi-form households only

SPECIMEN

### To the Householder, Joint Householders or members of the household aged 16 or over

The Census is a count every ten years of all people and households in the country. Census information is used by central and local government, health authorities and many other organisations to allocate resources and plan services for everyone. The Office for National Statistics conducts the Census in England and Wales.

### Completing your form

Completion of the Census form is compulsory under the Census Act 1920. If you refuse to complete it, or give false information, you may be liable to a fine. This liability does not apply to question 10 on religion. The requirement for you to return a completed form will not be satisfied until such a form has been received. If you need help, please contact the Census Helpline.

### Confidentiality

The information you provide is protected by law and treated in strict confidence. The information is only used for statistical purposes, and anyone using or disclosing Census information improperly will be liable to prosecution. Census forms will be held securely. Under the current terms of the Public Records Act 1958, the data will be treated as confidential for a period of 100 years.

### Thank you for counting yourself in.

*Len Cook*

national
**STATISTICS**

Len Cook
REGISTRAR GENERAL FOR ENGLAND AND WALES

### What you have to do

♦ Your household should complete this form in **black or blue ink**. A household is:

• one person living alone, or

• a group of people (not necessarily related) living at the same address with common housekeeping - sharing either a living room or sitting room, or at least one meal a day.

♦ This form covers five people. If there are more than five people in your household you will need an extra form.

♦ Identify household members in Table 1 (page 2). It will help you to complete the form if you use Table 2 to identify visitors.

♦ Answer the questions about your accommodation (page 3).

♦ Complete the relationship question (pages 4 and 5).

♦ Answer the remaining questions for every member of your household.

♦ Sign the Declaration and **post the form back** in the envelope supplied.

## Declaration

♦ To be signed after completing this form. Please check that you have not missed any pages or questions.

**This form is completed to the best of my knowledge and belief.**

**Signature/s**

**Date**

Page 1

*Part of the 2001 census form for England*

To get an overall picture and see how important care is as a form of work, we would need to add up all these people. But how could that be done? There are many different records that employers keep and statistics that they need to provide for government departments. Gathering relevant statistics and trying to compare them, however, can be a nightmare, even for a very experienced researcher. One place to start is with the census.

A census form comes through the letterbox once every 10 years. The householder is legally obliged to fill it in, listing each person over 18 in the household and giving – among many other things – a description of the occupation of each adult. Several shelves full of information from the most recent censuses can be found in major libraries. Results for England, Wales and Scotland appear in volumes labelled *Census of Great Britain*. Separate volumes are prepared for Northern Ireland. These results have been slow in appearing. Detailed tables from the 1991 census, for example, were still being published throughout the decade which followed. Now, however, things are beginning to speed up. The government statistics website will tell you the very latest information that is available (www.statistics.gov.uk/census2001/) [accessed 21.2.02].

What can we glean from the information on care-related occupations in the census? First, we need to decide which jobs are care work and which are not. In Unit 1 a definition of an informal carer was proposed as 'a person who takes unpaid responsibility for the physical and/or mental well-being of someone who cannot perform the tasks of daily living unaided, because of illness or disability'. A care worker, we might then say, is someone who does the same things on a paid basis. How complete a picture does this give of the whole care workforce?

Asking this question in 2002 meant that the detailed results for the 2001 census were not yet available. I had to go back to the 1991 tables. One of these tables is called 'Occupation and employment status, Great Britain' and runs to a total of 11 pages of small print (OPCS, 1994). It covers over 25 million people – all those aged 16 and over who had a paid job, were in training for a job or were seeking work. The questions asked for a description of the job a person held last week or the last job they had had – provided they had been employed in the last ten years. Spending some time on this table and examining it closely will help to clarify how very diverse the care workforce is and how tricky it is, even at this late stage in the course, to define a care worker adequately.

Nine main categories of occupation are used in the table. These are subdivided and subdivided again to give nearly 400 individual occupations or occupational groups. So where in this maze are the people we think of as care workers?

The nine main occupational groups are:

1    managers and administrators

**2    professional occupations**

**3    associate professional and technical occupations**

4    clerical and technical occupations

5    craft and related occupations

**6    personal and protective service occupations**

7    sales occupations

8    plant and machine operatives

9    other occupations.

**Table 1 Selected occupations in Great Britain, 1991 (10 per cent sample)**

| Professional occupations | |
| --- | --- |
| Health professionals: | |
| medical practitioners | 9,544 |
| pharmacists/pharmacologists | 2,566 |
| ophthalmic opticians | 691 |
| dental practitioners | 2,043 |
| veterinarians | (717) |
| *Total* | 14,844 |
| | |
| Professional occupations nec: | |
| psychologists | (698) |
| other social and behavioural scientists | (282) |
| clergy | 3,411 |
| social workers, probation officers | 10,296 |
| *Total* | 13,707 |
| **Associate professional and technical occupations** | |
| Health associate professionals: | |
| nurses | 48,432 |
| midwives | 3,200 |
| medical radiographers | 1,349 |
| physiotherapists | 2,014 |
| chiropodists | 860 |
| dispensing opticians | 353 |
| medical technicians, dental auxiliaries | 2,108 |
| occupational and speech therapists, psychotherapists etc. | 3,031 |
| environmental health officers | (874) |
| other health associate professionals nec | (752) |
| *Total* | 61,347 |
| | |
| Social welfare associate professionals: | |
| matrons, houseparents | 4,870 |
| welfare, community and youth workers | 9,739 |
| *Total* | 14,609 |
| **Personal and protective service occupations** | |
| Health and related occupations: | |
| assistant nurses, nursing auxiliaries | 15,693 |
| hospital ward assistants | 2,448 |
| ambulance staff | 2,195 |
| dental nurses | 2,856 |
| care assistants and attendants | 28,276 |
| *Total* | 51,468 |
| | |
| Childcare and related occupations | |
| nursery nurses | 5,925 |
| playgroup leaders | (1,957) |
| educational assistants | (4,248) |
| other nec | 19,211 |
| *Total* | 25,136 |
| *Total workforce\* in all the above occupational groups* | 181,111 |
| *Total workforce\* in Great Britain* | 2,591,497 |

\* Total workforce includes employees, self-employed, unemployed and students.
(Source: OPCS, 1994, pp. 16–27)

Care workers are to be found in categories 2, 3 and 6 (shown in bold type in the list). Table 1 shows the relevant subheadings under each of these three main groupings and the numbers of people working in each. Taking a brief look at the table:

- **Professional occupations** has a subgroup called 'health professionals'. This is where we find doctors, dentists, opticians and others. The broad heading of professionals finishes with a group 'nec' (meaning 'not elsewhere classified') and here we find social workers and also clergy.

- **Associate professional and technical occupations** has a health subgroup with 10 occupational groups, starting with nurses and including various therapists and others, and also a social welfare subgroup.

- **Personal and protective service occupations** is a very broad heading placing the armed forces, police and security officers ('protective' occupations) alongside the personal service jobs we are interested in. Occupations included in the table are subdivided into health and also into childcare jobs.

Some of those you may have listed as jobs for care workers in Activity 1 do not emerge clearly at all. I will come back to this shortly.

---

Activity 2    **Care work in the census 1**

*Allow about 15 minutes*    Table 1 is complicated and it is best to look at it in two parts. For this activity you will not need to look at the numbers.

(a)    Look at the names of the occupational categories in the table. They are grouped in the census categories that have just been explained. Put a tick against those that you would definitely include as hands-on care workers. (You might want to read again the definition of carers which was given earlier before you make your decisions.)

(b)    Next, looking at those census headings – 'health associate professionals' and so on – do you consider that they are a good way of grouping these different kinds of care workers?

(c)    Are there any other occupations that you would want to include in the list of care workers?

---

Comment    (a)    Decisions about whom to include and exclude are not straightforward. My suggestion is to exclude seven groups and I have put brackets round the numbers for these groups in the table and excluded them from the totals. I excluded vets and also psychologists, social scientists, environmental health officers and 'others' as not routinely doing care work directly with other people. This might be too drastic a decision – clinical psychologists, for example, should probably be in, and there is no way of knowing who is in the 'other' category who might have been included. I also excluded education assistants and playgroup leaders on the grounds that they should be counted in the sphere of education rather than the care sector.

Since numbers for all these excluded groups are small, these decisions will not make a great difference to the overall pattern of results. You should bear in mind, however, as you work through this section, that the figures are somewhat arbitrary.

(b) When considering who gets grouped in which category, you may have noticed that doctors, dentists, social workers and various others are regarded here as 'professionals', whereas nurses, midwives and therapists of different kinds are 'associate professionals', and other workers are regarded as being in personal service occupations. Also, there is a clear division between health and social care at the associate professional level, and one group of care workers, those who work with children, is listed separately in the personal service category. These distinctions say something about the prestige of different occupations and I will come back to this when I consider the meaning of 'profession' later in the unit.

(c) On the question of other occupations to include as care work, I had the advantage of being able to look through the full list of occupations. I could not easily find domestic staff in hospitals (you read in Unit 2 about domestic staff getting involved in patient care), but I found hospital porters grouped under 'other sales and service occupations' in classification 9. I wondered whether they should be included. I also considered undertakers, who were located in a miscellaneous category in personal and protective occupations. Owners of residential and nursing homes often take a direct part in care work, especially if they are registered nurses. They were in a broad grouping at the end of category 1 called 'managers and proprietors in service industries nec'. In other words they were in the miscellaneous category – and there was no way of knowing how big a proportion of it they formed! You may have thought of yet other groups – one of our testers insisted that she would class someone she knew who sold orthopaedic beds as a care worker. The census would put such a person firmly in category 7 as 'sales'.

Rather than memorise these odd-sounding census categories in any detail, the point is to remember that they are arbitrary. This is not necessarily the way occupations would be grouped if one were doing it today. In fact, there is a strong incentive to keep categories the same over many years so that long-term trends can be established. It is always worth pausing, however, to look at how the information has been grouped before turning to the findings of a table.

Activity 3 **Care work in the census 2**

*Allow about 10 minutes* If we accept the census definitions, what does Table 1 tell us about the care workforce?

(a) Which are the biggest groups of care workers?

(b) How important are care workers when compared with the workforce as a whole?

In answering these questions, bear in mind that the published table and hence the information reproduced here is based on analysing a 10 per cent sample of the total census returns. To get an approximation of the total numbers in the workforce, you need to add a nought to each figure – not 9,500 doctors but 95,000, and so on.

Comment (a) You can see something about the relative size of the different occupations just by inspecting the figures. Associate professionals are the biggest grouping, and nurses account for the greater part of it. There are nearly 50,000 nurses in this 10 per cent sample, therefore nearly 500,000 – nearly half a million – in the workforce in Great Britain as a whole. No other single occupational group comes anywhere near this figure, although if you look at the broader grouping called 'health and related occupations', it might be reasonable to say that care assistants of various sorts, if we put them together, would form a group of a similar size. There are close to 100,000 doctors and slightly more than this number of social workers, but all other occupations are very much smaller.

(b)   Adding all the groups in the table together gives a total of around 1.8 million people engaged in care work. With a total workforce of over 25 million (see the last line of the table), a quick calculation shows that care workers – as I have defined them here – comprise seven per cent of the total paid workforce. Although you cannot see it from the figures, that is about the same number as all those in the building trades and skilled engineering trades put together. So care work is a very significant form of work activity.

The table is undoubtedly useful in a number of respects. It shows clearly how some specialised health care occupations which are widely known and understood are actually quite small. There are small numbers of physiotherapists, radiographers, chiropodists and others compared with approximately 100,000 doctors and 100,000 social workers. And doctors and social workers themselves are a drop in the care workforce ocean compared with half a million nurses. But the table is also frustrating. It gives a much less clear picture of many of the caring jobs that we have been concerned with in this course. Terms like 'ward assistants' and 'auxiliaries' and groupings such as 'welfare, community and youth workers' do not neatly match job titles. It is harder to figure out what these categories mean and to try to establish over time whether the workforce as a whole is becoming less skilled, and whether the boundaries between health and social care are shifting. In the end, the census table answers some questions but raises others.

Of course, there are other ways to piece together information about the care workforce: for example, by separating out detailed statistics for health and social care staff. National Training Organisations for health and for social care, as we shall see later, worked on building an overall picture and this suggests that the figures are a lot higher than my census count. But, whatever statistical sources one tries to use, it still remains difficult to establish a good overall picture of the balance of different kinds of work and also of how that balance might be changing. Despite the size and importance of the care workforce, it has not been until very recently that policymakers have tried to consider it as a whole in the way I am trying to do in this section. *And if no one has been thinking about it as a whole, starting to plan for it as a whole is going to take time.*

## 1.2   Adding in the unpaid carers

A table of paid occupations in care says nothing about the unpaid caring work that family members do in the home. Women have often felt comfortable with describing their occupation as 'housewife' on any official form and with seeing caring as part and parcel of being a housewife. Men doing full-time caring, faced with a question about their occupation, would be more likely to respond that they were unemployed or retired than to describe themselves as carers. Once specific questions started to be asked in government surveys, however, the volume of unpaid caring work that was being undertaken began to emerge.

We may have thought that the paid health and social care labour force is large, as indeed it is. We have seen that it accounts for at least seven per cent of the paid workforce. But in the whole army of carers, it is only a battalion. One estimate is that *alongside a figure of approaching two million or so paid employees in health and social care work, are nearly seven million carers* (as you will see in the activity below). But we need to take care – the counting has been subject to much debate. And, of course, some people are in both groups – doing paid care then going home to do unpaid care for relatives.

*In the army of carers paid workers are only a battalion*

---

Activity 4    **How many unpaid carers?**

*Allow about 15 minutes*    There is controversy about how many informal carers there are. On some estimates the figure reaches nearly seven million, on others the figure is under two million. How can this enormous discrepancy be accounted for?

To answer this question you will need to do a revision exercise. Go back to Unit 1, Section 1.3, and skim-read the subsection entitled 'Duration and frequency'.

---

Comment    The first, large estimate of how many people were informal carers came in response to a question in the 1985 *General Household Survey* that asked whether people took on extra responsibility for someone sick, disabled or elderly. Around six million people said 'yes' to this. By the 1990 survey, the number had risen to 6.8 million. Unit 1 points out, however, that if we concentrate on just the main carers – who spend more than 20 hours per week on caring – then the figure is much smaller, around 1.5 million.

Which of these figures should we accept? Campaigners concerned with developing government policy to support carers have focused on the 1.5 million figure. These are people caring many hours a week, who can become isolated and exhausted, and whose own health can suffer in ways that were outlined in Section 3 on 'stresses and strains' of caring in Unit 1. The Carers National Association (CNA), a voluntary organisation formed to support carers and lobby government for change, took a different view. Early in the 1990s, its director commented:

> *It may be 1.7 or 1.4 million at the heavy end, but on the other hand there are a lot of people caring for someone in another household, for less than 20 hours a week, who have their lives restricted, and who are picking up the burden which the state is not.*

(Quoted in Redding, 1991, p. 20)

In the longer chapter from which your Reader Chapter 20 is drawn, Annie Bibbings – from the same organisation – discusses what more should be done for carers. She supports the CNA view and says that carers such as these:

> *... provide the bulk of community care support to frail, elderly people and children and adults with disabilities. Indeed they provide more care than health and social services and the voluntary and private sectors combined.*

(Bibbings, 1994, p. 159)

There is still more to find out about the hidden side of informal caring – just how much of it there is and who does it. The 1985 six million figure caused some surprise, since as many as 40 per cent of those who replied that they took on extra responsibilities were men. Prior to this, it had been assumed that the bulk of caring was done by women. Research then began to show that spouse care among older people was a particularly important category. Such care was being undertaken fairly equally by men for women and by women for men (Arber and Ginn, 1990). This brought the caring role of men more into focus (Bytheway and Johnson, 1998). However, some people have said that we still have not got a full estimate of women's caring work. Since the survey question asks about 'extra responsibility', it may well be that women under-report it; shopping for mother, dropping in to give her a hand, might be seen as so natural by women that they do not count it in the way that men do (Arber and Ginn, 1990; Parker, 1992). However, we can summarise that nearly seven million people say they are making *some* contribution to care (although sometimes only a small one) and approaching two million of them are playing a very substantial part in the care labour force without being paid for what they do. Caring, as Unit 1 reminds us, is certainly 'a family affair'.

Is that everyone accounted for? Not quite. *Volunteers* are an important category of unpaid workers in the care workforce. They also need to be considered. The website of the National Centre for Volunteering, based in London, is a mine of information (www.volunteering.org.uk [accessed 28.3.02]). When I visited it, I found that 22 million adults are involved in formal volunteering each year and that 90 million hours of formal voluntary work takes place each week. Not all of this is in the health and social care field, of course, but caring work is a significant form of volunteering and volunteering overall is on the increase. It is supported by government initiatives, like Millenium Volunteers, a turn of the century scheme to encourage young people to volunteer and The Experience Corps, a campaign launched in 2002 to recruit over 50s. Looking at the website, I also learned:

- how to keep up with research on volunteering – through the projects and publications of the Institute for Volunteering Research

- how organisations recruiting volunteers were being helped to attract volunteers from under-represented groups through 'Diversity Challenge'

- what the plans were for volunteers week – held in June each year to encourage more people to get involved

- how to become a volunteer in the health and social care field – there was a long list of voluntary organisations to contact.

Voluntary organisations in health and social care, as the list in the National Centre for Volunteering website shows, take many forms. Some are large fundraising, campaigning and service-delivery organisations that have a 100-year history behind them and employ considerable numbers of professional staff as well as volunteers. You met the children's charity Barnardo's in Unit 16. Others are small, local schemes, meeting a need, for example for befriending and supporting people who are unable to carry out daily activities unaided. Despite the ways in which voluntary organisations have changed, it seems from the website and from other research, that rates of volunteering have held up over time (Taylor, 1995).

*Right and overleaf: Prize-winning entries from the 1997* Guardian / *National Centre for Volunteering photographic competition*

*Winning way ... Patrick Merrifield's photograph of voluntary worker Rufus consoling a young boy in his charge during a day trip won first prize, capturing the trust between adult and child*

*'What's life without a laugh? ... runner-up was Thomas Jargensen's picture of Ralph receiving oxygen, showing his subject's zest for life*

*Golden shot ... Jon Cleaver's photograph of Ken, a tetraplegic, was third with its scene of an archery competition at a country sports day*

### Now we know that there are more

Two bodies were at work early in 2002, piecing together more of an overall picture of the paid element of the workforce in care and starting to plan more comprehensively for education and training. Healthwork UK was then the National Training Organisation (NTO) for the health sector. It estimated that in 2001 there were around *2 million* people working in health care – most working for the NHS, but as many as half a million or more working in the independent and voluntary sectors or in complementary and alternative medicine. In the social care field, TOPSS, the NTO for personal social services, calculated that in England alone, *another million* people work in social care, 60 per cent of them employed by local authorities. Overall, the workforce here is more fragmented. There are also 25,000 other employers – many are owners of residential homes often with very small numbers of staff. And unlike in health, where a high proportion are professionally qualified, TOPSS estimated that 80 per cent of the care workforce have no qualifications at all.

Since April 2002, NTOs no longer exist and new Sector Skills Councils are being developed. In the meantime the two organisations are continuing with their work but will be called Skills for Health and TOPSS until their new status is agreed.

If you have access to the internet, you might like to look at the websites below to see if there is more up-to-date information.

www.skillsforhealth.org.uk [accessed 29.8.02]

www.topss.org.uk [accessed 28.3.02]

In this section I have tried to answer the question 'who are the care workers?' As was clear in the first activity you carried out, the boundaries of care work are not easy to establish. Different decisions will be made about whom to include, depending on what people's purposes are. You might have noticed that the figures of around 3 million in total in the last box are very much higher than the 1.8 million paid workers I calculated from the census. And this 3 million leaves out unpaid carers and volunteers that I went on to discuss. All in all, it remains difficult to piece together the complete national figures on which planning for the care workforce can be based.

But however we look at the statistics, it is very clear that health and social care work is a significant component of the labour force and of our lives. So what training is available? Patterns of training for the paid members of this workforce is the key theme for the next section. Just what qualifications are open to care workers? Are these workers easily transferable between different areas of care work? You will look at two kinds of qualification, vocational and professional, and explore the hierarchy of skills in the workforce that this represents. To start with, the focus is on the idea of skill and how it relates to care.

---

**Key points**

- Very large numbers of people are engaged in caring work, the vast majority on an unpaid basis.
- The paid workforce in care is also large.
- The two biggest groups of paid carers are registered nurses and care assistants of various kinds.
- Governments have only recently begun to think about planning for this workforce as a whole.

# Section 2

# Is caring skilled work?

We have seen that a large proportion of the care workforce carries out care on a paid basis but without being members of the established care professions or going through a lengthy training. You have certainly met a number of such workers in studying this course. Some, like Ann, the health care assistant at Leeds General Infirmary, work as part of a team under the supervision of a registered nurse in a hospital (Unit 2). Others, in residential homes like Liberty of Earley House (Unit 8), form the core of the staff, with advice and support from the care professions as needed. Still others, like Mary and Sue (Unit 3), although they have seniors to whom they can refer, are mainly working on their own in clients' homes. How skilled does someone who works in the homes of others as a carer need to be? In the examples we are about to consider, Lucy works as a nursing auxiliary, part of the district nursing service. She has the support of a qualified district nurse. The work that she does, however, increasingly overlaps with that provided by social services departments and by private agencies who supply home care. We will consider the skills of these different home carers together.

## 2.1  Paid carers talking about care work

Activity 5

*Allow about 30 minutes*

**The skills of a home carer 1**

Read Offprint 33 which focuses on Lucy as she carries out her daily work. For this activity you are asked to imagine that you are setting up a training programme for people beginning to do home care work. What kinds of things might you put in your notebook about the skills Lucy is using? See if you can make a note of Lucy's skills in relation to each client she visited.

(You might notice from the offprint that Lucy is working towards vocational qualifications. I will come back to the vocational qualifications system later in the unit.)

Comment

Your notebook might read something like this.

**Visit 1**: Lucy assesses the risk in an ambiguous situation. Makes an autonomous judgement, reschedules her time.

**Visit 2**: Lucy needs to operate an electric hoist for this severely disabled client (how many models and varieties of lifting equipment is she familiar with?). She shows knowledge of wound care (of how many different kinds?). She is competent in male catheterisation as a procedure, she knows how to carry out intimate care without embarrassment to either party. She communicates sensitively with the carer – perhaps it was Lucy who taught Mrs White about care of pressure areas.

**Visit 3**: Lucy takes an important initiative here in deciding to focus on the carer. She has a lot of information about services and entitlements for clients and for their carers.

**Visit 4**: Lucy does not only know about the statutory services – she has put this couple in touch with a relevant voluntary body, the MS Society.

**Visit 5**: Lucy knows about Alzheimer's disease and the strains it puts on close relatives. She has taken a decision about what leaflets to carry with her – the state Sally was in, there is no way she would have taken information in if Lucy had just mentioned it.

**Visit 1** (again): another adjustment to the plan here. Lucy is able to identify and respond to her client's moods. She has managed a difficult client and averted a potential confrontation – conflict management is a skill she has.

Lucy's morning certainly brings home the wide range of skills and knowledge she needs to care for people in their own homes. But job descriptions do not always cover the full range of what carers are expected to do, and carers themselves often tend to play down the skills they possess. A revision exercise will help to take this further. Find Unit 3 in Block 1 and turn to Section 3, 'Labour or love? Home carers'.

Activity 6    **The skills of a home carer 2**

*Allow about 20 minutes*

Reread Sections 3.1 and 3.2 of Unit 3 as far as the heading 'Limitations to friendship'. Then reread Section 3.3 as far as the heading 'Training and induction'. Do this reading quickly. Do not listen to the audio again – the Comment sections will remind you of some of the things Mary, a home carer working for a privately owned home care service, said. Mary is very positive about her job, but at the same time she plays down her skills. See if you can note down *how* this happens and find what Unit 3 suggests about *why* it happens.

Comment    How does Mary play down her skills? Her job is probably not unlike Lucy's but she talks about her personal relationships with clients rather than her skills in meeting their needs. In doing this, Mary is ignoring the nursing skills she has learnt, she is not noticing the assessments she makes and the knowledge she has to offer. She is equating an array of interpersonal skills with being 'like family'.

Why does this happen? Unit 3 suggested that socially important work like caring is seen in the wider world as unskilled or semi-skilled and is accorded little economic value.

It is all too easy to undervalue the skills that carers use. People like Mary and Lucy are not highly paid (see the box below). Often they have had very little training. Recruitment literature, induction sessions and training days for care assistants tend to draw parallels between the caring in the job and the caring new recruits have already done in a family. This can help to build a new home carer's confidence but it also gives the message that the job does not have real skills attached to it. Also, formal job descriptions – as Unit 3 showed – tend to talk about the skills needed as if they were personal qualities that 'anyone' might possess (humour, warmth, or perhaps maturity, for example).

---

**What does a care assistant earn?**

Jobs in home care and residential care – along with jobs as health care assistants, nursing auxiliaries and support workers in hospitals – are among the lowest paid of all. Legislation creating a National Minimum Wage came into force in 1998. This has improved the situation – though not as much as some would like. Research commissioned by the trade union UNISON calculated that average earnings were well below the Council of Europe decency threshold and were hovering around half the national average. The study involved focus groups and interviews with non-registered nurses in four trusts across the UK. It concluded that these experienced workers, increasingly in the front line of care and substituting for registered staff, were not getting the recognition they deserved. Many simply couldn't make ends meet.

> "I'm a main earner, as my husband was made redundant recently. We had our phone cut off, we're just broke. Recently the car needed work, but you just can't afford to pay for any extras."

> "I do bank shifts ... I've also had to do all the overtime, night shifts etc I can get to help pay off my overdraft."

> "I recently married and we're now expecting a child, but we're so short of money ... I'm still paying the wedding off!"

(Thornley, 2001, pp. 23-4 [quoted with permission]; see also Thornley, 1997)

Jobs that make assumptions about skills that women have developed through the work they do as mothers, daughters and partners in and for families have been called 'gendered jobs' (Davies and Rosser, 1987). Many jobs which involve contact with others – secretarial work, reception work, sales assistants, customer liaison, as well as caring work like home care and nursing – are like this. To call jobs 'gendered' in this way is not to say that men do not sometimes do these jobs and do them well. It is to say that these jobs have assumptions about 'women's natural skills' built into them and that people recruiting for these jobs take for granted the skills that their largely female applicants bring. Thus, they do not need formally to train people or to reward them highly for what seem to be natural qualities. We all have had some informal training in care but because it happens in the home we do not tend to think of it as skill.

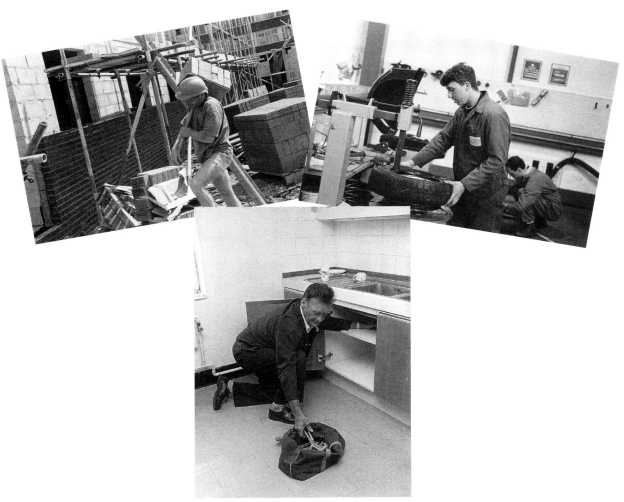

*Some of the traditional skilled trades*

Think for a moment about two ideas: a 'skilled man' and a 'skilled woman'. Most people would probably recognise the collage of pictures here. Jobs such as welder, plumber, motor mechanic, carpenter, millwright, electrician and bricklayer are well known examples of the trades or crafts of the skilled man. Jobs in these areas have been dwindling, traditional apprenticeships are changing, but the images are still fairly familiar. Could we put together a similar collection of images for the skilled woman? Strictly speaking, you might say 'yes'. We could include skills in the textile trade – dressmaking and millinery for example – we could include hairdressing, and we might want to point out that women are increasingly becoming carpenters, plumbers, and so on. And yet the concept of a 'skilled woman' does not sound quite right. The commonsense understanding of skill – the historical legacy with which we work – is of skill as involving manual labour, working with tools and on materials, taking place in a workplace and to do with the creation of products. All this makes it easy to downgrade the skills that women often use, especially skills in caring, as the cartoon implies.

## 2.2 Techniques for teasing out women's skills at work

Agencies with an interest in creating greater equality between the sexes in employment – such as the Equal Opportunities Commissions for Britain and its Northern Ireland equivalent, trade unions and women's campaigning groups – have been rethinking and broadening concepts of skill. The next box is drawn from a joint government and trade union project in South Australia. The aim was to describe much more accurately the skills women used in clerical work and ultimately to recognise and reward women for the work they do.

The authors realised that they could not simply ask women what skills they used. This would just reinforce the existing devaluation of women's work. Instead, ways had to be found of working actively with women to uncover what was hidden and taken for granted. This involved building trust and respect, encouraging women to find ways of describing their responsibilities and working with them to explore and develop their statements. Out of this came some guidance – how *not* to describe your job if you want to recognise what skills you are actually using! (These headings may be familiar – they were used in Unit 5 as a way of helping you to start thinking about your own skills.)

---

**Six guidelines for evaluating women's work**

1   **Avoid minimising**. Women may discount skills they have acquired through informal means, understate the complexities of work that they are extremely competent at or enjoy, and fail to claim skills that are used irregularly or when standing in for a colleague. Sentences that start 'I just ...', 'I only ...', 'I do a bit ...' should ring warning bells. They are indications of the minimising of skills.

2   **Be specific about tasks and skills**. Using broad terms like interpersonal skills and being a teamworker or good communicator can imply that activities are less skilled than they actually are. There is a need for careful consideration of the full range of skills. Don't assume that the lowest level of skill is being used, and where work involves contact with

the public, look out for skills in resolving conflict. These are important tips since factors such as these are often missed.

3 **Describe skills not personality**. Many of the skills which women workers have get described as personal attributes – (you have to 'like people', 'have broad shoulders', 'be easy-going', 'discreet', 'adaptable' ...). The rule here is to avoid assuming some things come naturally and to translate 'being' words into 'doing' ones ('I welcome customers ...', 'I listen ...', 'I tolerate ...', 'I co-operate with ...', 'I maintain a calm manner ...').

4 **Recognise industry knowledge**. When people say that they use their 'common sense', 'instinct' or 'general experience', this often means that they have a detailed knowledge of the organisation and the sector. Skills are still skills even if women have learnt them by being 'just dropped in the deep end', or by 'only picking it up as I went along'.

5 **Value responsibility accurately**. Responsibility for money or machines often gets a high rating in job descriptions and job evaluations, whereas responsibility for the satisfaction of customers or the welfare of clients is noticed less. Also, the work that women do is often described as routine work or support, where the formal responsibility remains with someone higher in the hierarchy. Here we need to ask exactly what it is that the worker does and what skills are needed for it.

6 **Include all tasks and skills**. It is important not to miss tasks that are allocated 'on the hoof' ('just look after our new recruit'), and things that are done on a voluntary basis: organising cards, presents and celebrations seems like an optional extra, but it also helps to create a harmonious workplace and a productive work team.

*(Adapted from South Australian Department of Labour, Women's Adviser's Unit, 1992, pp. 15–37)*

---

Activity 7 **Rethinking care work and its skills**

*Allow about 20 minutes*

Do you feel that any of these guidelines might apply to the work of:

(a) a member of a hospital's domestic staff?

(b) a care assistant in a residential home for old people?

(c) work that you yourself do (paid or unpaid)?

Take *one* example from this list and compose a statement that such a person might make (or that you yourself have made), falling into some of the traps set out in the box. Try to cover at least three.

---

Comment

All of us, men or women, are likely to underestimate what it takes to do work that we are very familiar with. We often just get on with the job without reflecting on it, and after years of experience it does feel that the work just 'comes naturally'. You have probably had the experience too of being the newcomer and finding that you are constantly asking how things are done, whom to contact, whether there is a procedure, and so on. At times like this it becomes clear just how much the 'old hands' take for granted.

Care work, along with clerical and secretarial work and other jobs that women do, often in support roles to others with more formal qualifications, can be particularly difficult to put into words. It is often taken for granted that women are 'good at interpersonal stuff'. Remember how in Unit 2 even for nursing – with its lengthy education and training – work has been necessary to bring 'emotional labour' into the open and acknowledge its importance.

This section has taken the argument in Unit 3 about the undervaluing of caring skills a stage further. It has been suggested that care work is associated with 'gendered' jobs, which are seen as falling 'naturally' to women. As a result and because the concept of skill is so closely associated with male manual work and manufacturing, the many skills involved in caring are simply taken for granted. These skills are seen as personal qualities that women are either born with or acquire as part and parcel of life in the home. This kind of thinking has led to a widespread devaluing of work done by women. Consequently, special efforts are needed to tease out skills of caring which have long gone unnoticed. An important step in this direction has been the establishment of vocational qualifications in care. We will explore this in the next section.

---

### Key points

- Caring is one of a number of 'women's jobs' which are not traditionally thought of as skilled. Such jobs often seem to need 'just common sense' or 'the right personality'.

- This is in part because the formal recognition of work-based skills has been associated with men's manual work in manufacturing.

- Unless we can identify skills it is unlikely that people can be fully trained or properly rewarded for them.

# Section 3
# Vocational Qualifications in care

What are vocational qualifications (VQs) and how have they developed in relation to caring work? What advantages and disadvantages do they have? I will start to answer these questions with an account of what was happening in one particular residential care setting which I visited in 1997 and again five years later.

## 3.1 VQs in one care setting

*Lathbury Manor residential home*

Lathbury Manor is a private residential home. Opened in 1990, it caters for 24 residents. Its imposing Georgian frontage, wide entrance hall and sweeping staircase are reminders of the past. As its name implies, it was once a grand house in the tiny hamlet of Lathbury, which is near Newport Pagnell in Buckinghamshire. The residents are mostly elderly people. When I first visited, Gillian Broadway, the owner, explained that she saw it as 'a home for life'. Some people have significant physical needs, others have dementia and need support in their everyday living. In the first section of Audio Cassette 7 you will hear Gillian explaining what she felt were the qualities a carer needed and why she was such an enthusiast for the system of training through vocational qualifications in care.

---

**Activity 8**

*Allow about 20 minutes*

### Why implement VQs?

Listen to the first section of Audio Cassette 7, side 1, and jot down your answers to the following questions.

(a) How does Gillian describe her own personal enthusiasm for VQs?

(b) Gillian claims there is a sound business case for a private home owner like herself implementing VQs. What is that case and what are her reasons for thinking that other home owners will disagree?

(c)   What does Gillian believe is distinctive about a VQ in care and what does she think it can achieve? (Note how she questions the idea that some people are just 'natural' carers and that skill does not come into it.)

---

Comment    (a)   Gillian gives two reasons why she is in favour of a system of VQs. One is her own background and her commitment to enabling other people to grow and develop through lifelong learning experiences. She clearly gets a lot of satisfaction from contributing to the growth of others. (In fact, although she does not say it here, she herself missed out on educational opportunity in her early years. She did an Open University degree and before opening the home ran literacy and numeracy classes giving a second-chance educational opportunity to adults.) Her second point is that VQs promote greater acceptance of what she calls 'the profession of carer' and give opportunities for career progression in an area that has not previously been seen as important.

(b)   Gillian feels that the VQ system provides a structure covering all the aspects that staff need to learn to provide good quality care – a ready-made framework for training. Also, in her experience, trained people give a lot back: they stay in the job longer, they get involved in decision making in the home. Three reasons she gives why other home owners may not be enthusiastic about VQs are: (i) because they feel they are an expensive outlay if people leave after six months, (ii) because VQs give staff tools for criticism which owners may not be able to respond to, and (iii) because some owners are not up to date and aware of what she calls the 'philosophy of care'; they do not understand that good practice means moving away from following routines and, instead, individualising the care that residents receive.

(c)   Caring is different from plumbing, Gillian says, because it is 'not so objective'. There is a sense in which carers know how to care already but a VQ means 'doing what you do better'. A care VQ thus builds on experience, confirming the competences and underpinning knowledge that people already have and links them to nationally agreed standards. In some ways she does seem to be saying that caring is something that 'comes naturally', or at any rate that we all have some experience of it. But what she is looking for is someone with experience of life and some personal qualities and motivation that she can develop.

A little of the history of VQs will be helpful at this point. A national VQ system has been in place since the mid-1980s. It aims to cover all kinds of work, although the original impetus was to improve skills in the manufacturing sector and to make Britain more productive and competitive in the world. From the outset, the plan was:

- to design qualifications that were directly relevant to the needs of employers
- to make training more open, flexible and accessible to all
- to increase the proportions of people in the workforce who were skilled
- to create a single system out of a wide array of complex, sometimes overlapping formal qualifications.

**National vocational qualifications – what? when? and why?**

The year 1986 marked the start of what has been called the 'skills revolution' in the UK with the setting up of a National Council for Vocational Qualifications (NCVQ). The Council's role was to create a unified and comprehensive system of work-related qualifications and to explain, promote and develop it. The aim was to enable people to add qualifications when and where they wished and to transfer them between employers and also between sectors. While the VQ system as established at that point covered all the UK, Scotland had a separate Council (SCOTVEC) that worked independently and indeed was set up slightly earlier than the NCVQ. That is why you will sometimes find references to both NVQs and SVQs. I will just refer to VQs to cover the system overall.

The NCVQ had no legal powers to impose a new pattern, so it had to find ways to work with interested parties, including employers, trade unions, the professions and the many training and awarding bodies already in existence. There has been a bewildering number of developments and adjustments stemming from this.

So what do things look like now? At the government level, policies for education and vocational qualifications are coming more closely together. For example, in England, the Department of Education became the Department for Education and Employment in 1995, and in 1997 was renamed the Department for Education and Skills. Both school and work-based qualifications are now under its wing. In 1995, the NCVQ was replaced by the much broader-based Qualifications and Curriculum Authority (QCA). This body sets the overall standards and funds much of the development work. In 2000, it started work for the first time on a National Qualifications Framework – mapping out and reducing the total number of qualifications available at different levels (see p. 59). And then there were the UK-wide National Training Organisations – lead bodies with a strong employer presence, developing the specific occupational standards for the workforce which VQs are designed to test. You met the care sector and health sector NTOs in Section 1 (see p. 20–21), where I noted the work they had been doing on workforce numbers. A shake-up of NTOs happened in Spring 2002 – the overall total of 70 for the economy as a whole was to come down to about 25 new Sector Skills Councils. What had been the health and social care NTOs in England remained as standard setting bodies though under different names and structures (see p. 20–21). And in the other parts of the UK, the care sector training organisations and the regulatory and registering bodies (to be discussed later, see p. 47) brought their functions together. Throughout all these changes, the original goals remained the same – to improve the quality of industry and public services, to make sure people have access to high quality education and training and to rationalise and simplify provision. A decade and more of developments has opened up opportunity and started to bring more coherence – but it is still remarkably difficult to keep up with changes and find your way around the maze.

If you need to know more, *Getting a Vocational Qualification: A K100 Student's Guide* sets out details for you, including details of arrangements in Scotland, Wales and Northern Ireland. Also you might like to visit the website of the Department for Education and Skills. You will find a lot of information telling you what VQs are, explaining the history, and describing key organisations. A 'what's new?' button helps to keep people up to date.

www.dfes.gov.uk/nvq [accessed 30.3.02]

The box gives you some background on VQs and a glimpse of just how much change there has been in the way they are organised and managed. From the outset of the VQ system, *lead bodies* with strong employer representation were set up for each industry sector. Their task was to analyse jobs, set occupational standards and identify components of skill needed. This way the training could be tailored to fit employer requirements in each sector. *Competence-based* training was the watchword: people were to learn in the workplace and to be assessed actually doing the job. Book knowledge was played down and written exams were out.

Setting up a lead body for care work was quite a challenge. It had to span the health sector, social services and local government. There were voluntary sector employers and there were private commercial residential homes such as Lathbury Manor. There were different care groups to think of: older people, children, people with learning difficulties, people with mental health problems, and so on. Although many care workers had no training to speak of and no qualifications, the range of agencies offering training and the array of certificates were mind-boggling.

Providing competence-based training leading to the award of a VQ was equally challenging. How were employers to find the time, the space and the skills to do it? And if it was going to be possible to spell out competences for different levels – would it be possible to go all the way from care assistant to social worker, nurse or doctor?

Let us break off here and listen to how competence-based education and training was working in Lathbury Manor on my first visit in the late 1990s. Gillian Broadway was a VQ assessor as well as the home owner. You will hear her in conversation with Ros, a care assistant who had worked at Lathbury Manor for about a year. Gillian quickly recognised her potential and encouraged her to start on a VQ. In order to give you a sense of what the VQ system means in action, I asked them to carry out a review of where Ros had got to in her VQ training and what the next steps were.

Activity 9    **VQs in action**

*Allow about 20 minutes*    Listen now to section 2 of Audio Cassette 7, side 1.

(a)    Throughout the interview Gillian reinforces important messages about what VQs are and about the underlying values on which they are based. Can you pick out at least two occasions when she does this?

(b)    The discussion highlights what Ros must do in working towards a VQ – she has not been sitting in a classroom, she has certainly not had to do TMAs! Make a list of each task she mentions.

Comment  (a)  One thing that Gillian does early on is to ask Ros whether her VQ experience has reassured her about what she knows and how competent she is. By saying 'you might not have to add much', she is seeking to build Ros's confidence. She is making Ros realise that she already understands a lot about care – partly because of her own life history and partly because of the role models she has around her. Later, when they are talking about Ros's food and drink project, Gillian listens to what Ros says she has learnt, then highlights the VQ values by saying that consulting the residents gives them control over their lives. Later still, when Ros says what she would do in the face of an abusive resident, Gillian introduces the possibility that inaction might be the best action. 'Maybe nobody can deal with it,' she says, and she indicates that the important thing is 'to leave him safe'.

(b)  There are several clues in this interaction as to what can be involved in doing VQs. Ros has taken *learning packs* away and studied them (Gillian mentioned these earlier), but has also taken part in *training sessions* based on them. She is very much in favour of this. You are not just going through it 'page by page', she says, instead you have an opportunity to talk. She has been set a *project* of consulting residents on how food and drink at Lathbury Manor compares with food and drink at home. Gillian teases out what she has learnt from this and adds to it. With the VQ elements on bathing, her *practice* was observed and Gillian, as assessor, asked her questions about her underlying thinking. In her forthcoming unit about abuse, the same process was about to take place, but here Ros was going to need to *write* notes about an incident she was involved in and discuss them with a view to entering these in her *portfolio*.

Not every VQ candidate will go through the exact process discussed here. The learning packs and training sessions based on them are something Gillian herself devised in her role as an assessor, and other assessors may do things differently. Gillian still uses her own learning packs, though compared with 1997, there are now many more books and other commercially available materials. It is clear from the exchange you have just heard, however, that a VQ measures competence – the ability to perform, to a nationally agreed standard, in a working situation. It is not just about what candidates *know*, but about what they *can do*.

**EVIDENCE SHEET**                                        Log No..03....

UNIT: Z10
ELEMENTS: A b + C .
DATE: 7-3-97
TIME:                                    **Evidence gathering method(s) used:**
    N.S.                                              ①

| RANGE COVERED | O Unit Reference |
|---|---|
| N.S. has very bad ARThiNtis, which gives her limited movement in her hands and body. N.S. is able to toilet and wash her hands her self. So this is usually done by her when it comes to meal times. N.S. takes her breakfast in her Room on a tray. which I take down to her. This IS set out on the tray with a tray Dolie and N.S. has freshly squesed orange Juce, wheetabix and all bran, Maralade Sandwich and an apple. N.S. use cutlery with thick handles and curved tops. She is able to feed her self. N.S. does not have a cup of tea at breakfast time as she likes to have this at 6.30am. I help N.S with her medication at breakfast time. She likes to have the tabdes placed on her tongue and she takes water from a glass with a straw. N.S also takes tatalose at breakfast time. to take this She tilts her reclaine chair right back to take the liquid down as she finds it very difficult to ka back due to her arthritis. The chair is then put back in the upright postia and then she takes water | O·e  Oc  Z19 |

*In 1997, Ros Gallop prepared a portfolio for her VQ award and also completed a Learning Pack designed at Lathbury Manor to relate to specific NVQ requirements and to involve few writing skills. The Unit details changed in 1998, but the overall emphasis remains the same* after making sure that N.S has everything that she needs and is comfortable I leave the room and so she can eat her breakfast.

Performance Criteria

| ELEMENT | RANGE | 1 | 2 | 3 | 4 | 5 | 6 | 7 | 8 | 9 | 10 | 11 | 12 | 13 | 14 | |
|---------|-------|---|---|---|---|---|---|---|---|---|----|----|----|----|----|---|
| 210 A | Hot + cold | ✓ | ✓ | ✓ | ✓ | | | | | | | | | | | |
| 210 B | cutlery special | ✓ | ✓ | ✓ | ✓ | ✓ | ✓ | | ✓ | ✓ | ✓ | ✓ | ✓ | ✓ | | |
| 210 C | Hot + cold cutlery Special | ✓ | ✓ | ✓ | ✓ | ✓ | ✓✓ | ✓ | | | ✓ | ✓ | | | | |
| | | | | | | | | | | | | | | | | |
| | | | | | | | | | | | | | | | | |
| | | | | | | | | | | | | | | | | |

<u>Comments by Assessor / Observer</u>        <u>Competent</u>

Ros prepared the tray accord to NS wishes. She is a lady who needs to have things done with meticulous detail. Ros recognises this, a was particular aware of her needs both - the choice of food - preparation. She communicated in a warm friendly manner bep courteous a responsive.

Signed: *G.E. Broadway.*
          ASSESSOR.

Date: 7.3.97

Name / role

Two other features of VQs are important at this stage. One has to do with values and the introduction of a values unit which candidates study whatever the level of VQ they are attempting and whatever their area of practice.

You have met the values idea in the six skills units in this course, since we drew on VQ values in designing them. These are the five values that Gillian had in mind:

1   promoting anti-discriminatory practice
2   maintaining the confidentiality of information
3   promoting and supporting individuals' rights and choices
4   acknowledging personal beliefs and identity
5   ensuring effective communication.

These values remain important, although after 1998 they changed somewhat and became known as Principles of Good Practice. Communication also became a full unit of its own at that point. (For more details, see *Getting a Vocational Qualification: A K100 Student's Guide.*)

The second important feature of VQs more generally is about levels. Ros, as well as Sheila, whom you will hear in the last section of side 1 of the audio cassette, was taking a VQ at level 2. In all sectors, VQs are assigned to one of five levels (although not all levels are used in all sectors). Because these levels cover all kinds of work, they are necessarily described in a very broad and abstract way. Level 1 had been eliminated in the care sector early on - on the grounds that care work was never entirely routine. I spoke to VQ assessor and K100 tutor, Sue Cusworth, about how the other levels related together (see box).

---

**Levels of work in care: an assessor explains**

Celia: Can you tell me what level 2 is – what does it mean someone can do?

Sue: *I explain to people that it is the basic practice level – you ought to be able to describe the work that you do and the thinking that underpins it. As an assessor, I will want to be able to observe you using your skills in daily practice.*

Celia: What about levels 3 and 4 then?

Sue: *At level 3 you are going to work more independently or have some supervisory responsibility – it might be that you are supervising people or it might be that you have responsibility for allocating resources. You need to be more able to reflect on your job and to be someone who actively promotes good practice. This level can now also give you entry to pre-registration training as a nurse. At level 4 you are likely to be someone who writes the policy and makes sure it is implemented. And above that – before you ask me! – you are likely to have responsibility for a whole area of services and you need to think more strategically about how things are developing.*

Celia: So does it link to educational qualifications?

Sue: *Yes and no. Broadly speaking you might want to say that level 2 is pitched at GCSE, level 3 at A level and level 4 at the first year of a degree and level 5 at graduate level. But for many people that kind of thinking probably isn't helpful – the whole point of VQs, after all, is about what you are able to do. And with good support, people are able to move up the skills ladder further than they would think if we started comparing them to graduates.*

Whatever the level you are working at, trying to understand how individual VQs are made up can feel daunting. At each level VQ awards are broken down into a number of *units of competence* to be achieved. Within the unit are *elements* that go to make up the unit, with *performance criteria* that determine what would constitute competent performance. What do care workers make of all this? I spoke to:

- *Ros*, whom you have just heard in discussion with Gillian

- *Maureen*, who not only completed a level 3 VQ but was on the way to becoming a trained VQ assessor

- *Sheila*, who has come from a very different background in caring for her husband at home and is carrying out a level 2 VQ.

Maureen, who has been in the VQ system a couple of years, had noticed how it has changed and become more streamlined (something she was clearly thankful for). She was also able to see it from both sides: you will hear her sympathise with 'the girls', when the language seems to make no sense at all to them!

---

Activity 10 | **Care workers' evaluations of VQs**
---|---

*Allow about 20 minutes*

Listen to the third and final section of Audio Cassette 7, side 1 now. How do these three carers evaluate VQs?

(a)   Make a note of what VQs have done for them as individuals.

(b)   Summarise the difference they think the training has made to the care they offer to the residents.

(c)   What else do they say about the experience of going through the process?

---

Comment

(a)   All three are certainly very positive about the personal impact of their VQ experience. Ros says that she is now more outgoing and has come out of her shell. Maureen feels that she was lucky at her time of life to get the chance to take this on, and Sheila, although she has done caring work before and is now caring on an unpaid basis for her husband at home, starts off by saying that this year at Lathbury Manor has turned her life around, opened her eyes and made her think.

(b)   Ros is clear that she has learnt good practice. She says that she now has more respect for older people. She knows how to do things like lifting properly and recently had a flash of understanding of what the value units really meant. Maureen talks about a 'deeper knowledge' and grasping the 'finer details', but it is Sheila who talks most about how different her practice is now. Before, she would just do things for people, whereas now she thinks about what they might want and she asks. She points out how hard it is to put all this into words – 'it's a matter of small things, and the learning pack looks common sense' but 'just because you've always done it this way, doesn't mean that it's right, or right for that person'.

(c)   Both Ros and Sheila show relief that doing VQs is not like going back to the classroom. 'There's no best handwriting or correct spelling,' says Sheila. Maureen was obviously thrown in the deep end: she says that it took her nine months to get into it, that she was terrified, and that the jargon didn't mean a thing. She can sympathise with the beginners now; she knows how they feel and encourages them to own up when they are mystified – for example, about PCs (performance criteria).

It was clear that Gillian's enthusiasm for VQs had rubbed off, at least on these three members of her staff. At the time of my first visit, Lathbury Manor was still a rather special place as far as VQs were concerned in having an owner who had taken part in developing them and who was herself an assessor for her staff. Five years on, when I revisited Lathbury Manor, I asked Gillian what had happened to her staff and and whether the system of VQs had improved overall.

---

**Where are they now?**

Returning to Lathbury Manor, I found that Ros and Sheila had left. Maureen was still there. She was now a VQ assessor in her own right. She had also become deputy manager of Park House, a sister home. Other staff had similar success stories. Gillian told me with great pride that three had gone on to do an access course for nursing and were now on the way to registered nurse status. Two others had successfully completed K100 and were on a pathway to degrees with The Open University. One of those budding nurses had recently written a letter to Gillian. 'I wouldn't have done it if you hadn't given me the confidence', she said. Perhaps the VQ system should take some of the credit too.

---

Next, we need to ask about how the system as a whole is working and to consider the critics as well as the enthusiasts.

## 3.2 Evaluating VQs in care

Activity 11

**The pros and cons of VQs**

Allow about 15 minutes

Here is a quotation taken from a statement by John Hillier, Chief Executive of the NCVQ, in an annual report some years ago.

> ... NVQs give everyone a chance to set and achieve personal goals. Progression and development can now take place as the individual chooses, in the area of work they select and at a pace to suit them — and it provides the possibility of moving back into education if that is the chosen route. No doors are barred nor opportunities removed to self-development.
>
> (NCVQ, 1993–4)

Judging from what you have heard about Lathbury Manor, and drawing from any relevant experience you might have had, do you agree with John Hillier's positive assessment as far as care VQs are concerned?

---

Comment

John Hillier is right that on paper the VQ system is accessible to everyone. Employees can start where they are in the workplace (or, for many women, from where they were before they took a career break) and build up their qualifications, moving through modules and levels at their own pace. In principle, too, unemployed people can join a programme that gives them a VQ in an area where they are most likely to get a job.

In practice, however, a potential VQ candidate might find a number of hurdles to entry and unsatisfactory practices in the system. Here are some of the criticisms that testers made in response to this activity.

*'No one talks about VQs in my workplace! I have tried to raise it but the interest just isn't there.'*

*'Lathbury Manor sounds a bit special – I found it hard to get my manager to give me time for it, and when your assessor comes in from the outside, things don't always go so smoothly linking up what you are actually doing with the VQs.'*

*'Progression and development? I'd like Mr Hillier to show me how that works. No one offered me more pay after I got the VQ or showed me what the next career step would be.'*

*'VQs seem to me to be just so much jargon. I can't make sense of it at all – I looked at it and thought "forget it!".'*

*'What if someone less clued-up than Gillian takes it on? If practice in the home is poor – all this workplace-based stuff means that you don't get the wider picture, doesn't it? You are not in contact with people who might criticise you. Can we be sure that standards are high in this VQ system and that they are the same everywhere?'*

Between them, these five testers raised key issues for the VQ system. Let us examine each in turn and see how things look after five more years.

1    'No one talks about VQs ...'

Accessibility is one of the central advantages put forward for the VQ system. You do not need to have formal educational qualifications, you can join in at any point in your working career, and you are building on what you already know. In 1997, some big employers were doing their own thing in training staff, and many small ones were not taking VQs on at all. 'There have been huge changes' said Gillian. 'With the arrival of the Care Standards Act 2000, 50 per cent of staff have to have a level 2 VQ and there is not one home owner who isn't aware of that and taking it on board'.

2    'Things don't always go so smoothly ...'

The practicalities of making VQ requirements fit a specific setting are not easy and staff may not have the resources, the skills or the time to do it. Gillian had an advantage from the start because she was a trained assessor who could assess VQs herself and show their relevance to the local setting. With a staff of around 40 (she owns two care homes), she had gone on to develop another senior carer to take on some of the training. Others are not so lucky. Releasing a group of staff to work with an outside or 'peripatetic' assessor can be a nightmare for a small home. 'How they are going to cope, financially and physically, I don't know', admitted Gillian.

3    'No one offered me more pay...'

The extent of recognition and reward is an important issue. At Lathbury Manor care assistants initially received a pay increase on obtaining their VQs. But Gillian found it caused difficulties with experienced staff who did not have the qualification and discontinued it. Care assistants' pay, as we saw earlier, remains low, and UNISON, while supporting more training, is also actively campaigning for more financial rewards and for greater recognition of skills that they see as still invisible (see the box, see also Thornley, 1997).

**A trade union perspective**

UNISON is the largest trade union in the health and social care sectors. There are more than 80,000 union members doing care assistant work in the health sector alone. I visited Unison official Paul Chapman, in May 2002, at the trade union headquarters in London and asked him what Unison thought about linking pay and qualifications. Should people get extra pay once they had gained a VQ? There needs to be a balance, he said, between rewarding growing experience in a job through incremental pay points each year and rewarding people who have demonstrated that they have extended their job-related competence through completing a relevant VQ. The topic had just been debated by members at their annual conference. Paul also told me about 'Agenda for Change' the government's initiative for modernising pay structures in the health service. And he gave me a copy of the union's current resource pack designed for health care assistants and non-registered nurses.

You can find out more by ringing Unison on 0800 5 97 97 50 or by going to Unison's website and tracking through the pages on health and nurses or on local government and social care.

www.unison.org.uk [accessed 11.5.02]

4     'Just so much jargon ...'

The *complexity* of the system and its *jargon* have been major causes for complaint, as you heard from Maureen on the cassette. It sometimes seems that terms change just for the sake of it. But it is

# Core no more in skills-go-round

Just when educationists think they are getting the hang of the technical vocabulary of vocational qualifications, bureaucrats go and change it all.

'Core skills' is to be phased out and replaced by 'key skills'. The six skills – sometimes also known as 'transferable skills' – will stay the same: communication, application of number, information technology, working with others, improving own learning, problem solving. But the 'core' part is being changed to prevent understandable confusion with 'core' units in NVQs, 'core' subjects in the national curriculum, and subject 'cores' within A level and AS level examinations.

(*Times Higher Education Supplement*, 19 July 1996, p. 1)

more likely that attempts to improve standards have been behind many of the changes that occur. Gillian was convinced that things had improved – guidance from the awarding bodies was better and all in all it was less heavy going these days.

5  'Can we be sure that standards are high ...?'

*Variable standards* has been a common criticism. Although external verifiers check on the standards that assessors work to, the system is not uniform. Assessment centres are resourced in different ways. This can lead to 'confusion and rivalry' between centres and hence serious variations in what should be a national quality standard (Dunlop, 1996). A mid-1990s survey indicated that as many as 38 per cent of assessors and an even higher proportion of external verifiers admitted to passing students who did not meet the standard (Eraut *et al.*, 1996). Again Gillian thought things had improved – guidance was stricter, assessment centres were inspected. The scandals that had led to criticism in the press and on TV in earlier years (Smithers 1994) do not seem to have been repeated.

An independent survey carried out in 1994 found that, like the staff at Lathbury Manor (and like Sue on Audio Cassette 1 for Unit 3), over half of candidates thought that working for a VQ helped them do their job better and approved of learning on the job. There was also considerable employer support (Toye and Vigor, 1994).

But perhaps Lathbury Manor was still ahead of the game. Five years ago, Gillian mused, there was a sense in which she was focused on VQs themselves and getting as many people through as time and money would allow. What was different now, she said, was that continued training was absolutely integral to the way of working. 'It's the ethos of the home – being a member of staff means taking on training.' She had recently started a new training round. Every staff member was going on a course on caring for vulnerable adults. At Lathbury, they had got the training habit and were making links with better standards even more than they had been doing five years ago.

> **Key points**
>
> • The VQ system provides qualification in caring based on competence assessed in the workplace rather than in a college setting. A range of different VQs in care at levels 2, 3 and 4 is now available.
>
> • On the positive side, VQs have identified and promoted skills in caring and have underlined the value base of caring work.
>
> • On the negative side, the system has faced a bewildering amount of change, Employer take-up has only recently been made compulsory and lack of uniformity in standards, bureaucracy and jargon have been criticised.
>
> • Linking of VQs to pay and career progression has begun, but care assistants report that there is still a long way to go before their skills are properly recognised and developed.

# Section 4
# Professions and professionalism

Those who see themselves as members of the professions in health and social care will be tempted to say that the education they receive is very different from the training that vocational qualifications offer and that there is an important difference between their work as professionals and the work of those who take vocational qualifications. But is there? And should there be? To consider this you need to think about what the terms 'profession' and 'professional' mean.

## 4.1 Dilemmas of definition

What exactly is a profession? Why is it that we are prepared to call some forms of work professions but we are unwilling to use the term for others? The term 'profession' often seems to give an occupation greater status and respect. But who decides this – and on what basis?

---

**Activity 12**

*Allow about 10 minutes*

**Everyday thinking about professions**

Think for a moment about some of the usual ways in which we use the terms 'profession', 'professional' and 'professionalism'. Below are six statements using some version of the word 'profession'. Jot down what you think is meant in each case.

(a) 'He's turned professional' (of a footballer).

(b) 'You really need some professional advice on this' (son to his father, who is making a will).

(c) 'What we have here is a member, shall we say, of the oldest profession' (police officer referring to a prostitute).

(d) 'Blocked drains? Call out the professionals' (advertisement in Yellow Pages).

(e) 'She acted like a real professional' (of a shop assistant dealing with an angry customer).

(f) 'Shall we keep this strictly professional?' (secretary to boss making a sexual overture at work).

---

**Comment**

There are a number of quite different ideas underlying these statements. Let us take them in turn.

(a) This is the distinction between the amateur and the professional – between someone who does something purely for enjoyment and someone who has chosen to make a living out of an activity and so is getting paid for it.

(b) This is perhaps the most established and conventional meaning of profession – an occupation (in this case law) which involves expert knowledge. This means that lay people are dependent on professionals, trusting them to give information and advice.

(c) This conveys much the same thing as (a), but there is a strong sense of irony because in this instance, the speaker is not according 'professional' status in the sense of (b).

(d) The advertisement claims that this firm can be trusted to do a competent job and meet the technical standards required.

(e)    This suggests an attitude or approach to the work, like keeping cool under pressure or adhering to a company rule which says 'never argue back'. There is something close to the meaning in statement (b) – this time not so much 'I am the expert with knowledge and skill', but 'you can trust me to behave calmly and objectively'.

(f)    This is different again; 'strictly professional' here means strictly work-related, although there is an implication too of proper codes of behaviour and an echo of the idea in (e), that is, of distancing emotion from role.

What this activity seems to tell us is that terms like profession and professional have passed into common currency. Being professional means many things – like being competent, being cool, keeping one's mind on the job and following proper procedures. But this gives us precious little help in deciding which occupations are professions. Indeed, it seems to suggest that whatever the job, people can behave in a professional manner. You may have noticed how Gillian Broadway used the term in just this way when she argued that the carers she employed in Lathbury Manor needed to be professional.

Although people often use terms loosely in this way, if we asked them to list occupations they thought of as professions, they would be unlikely to single out the shop assistant or the plumber. It is much more likely that they would come up with people like lawyers, doctors, architects and accountants. What do professional occupations like these have in common? And are they really so different from other occupations? I asked our course testers for reactions to this question. Their answers seemed to fall into two groups – those who clearly thought that professionals were different and in some way superior and those who thought otherwise.

---

Those who took a positive view:

- Professionals are the people we go to with major problems in life who have the special knowledge to deal with them.

- They are society's experts – they have spent long years of complex training. You can trust professionals to act in your best interests.

- They find out about you as well as your problems, they treat you as an individual. They are very committed to what they do and they really care.

Those who did not:

- They are the ones who have nice well-paid jobs and a comfortable middle-class lifestyle.

- They are the people who have conned us that they are more important than anyone else. They get together in professional associations which are just high-class trade unions, and they are really elitist too – they keep other people out.

- I always feel I am a 'case' with professionals – they sit there saying 'ah' and 'um' and 'really' and 'let me just check'. You never know what they really think.

## "FIFTY YEARS."

1838.                                                1888.

THEN.                                                 NOW.

**Supplement to the "NURSING RECORD," December 20, 1888.**

(The " Nursing Record " is Published every Thursday, Price 2d. Office, Dorset Works, Salisbury Square, Fleet Street, London.)

*Proprietors: SAMPSON LOW, MARSTON, SEARLE AND RIVINGTON (Limited).*

*Histories of professions often idealise progress*

The sociological study of professions has also reflected these 'pro' and 'anti' positions. Freidson, an American sociologist who has made a lifetime study of the medical profession and of the nature of medical knowledge, summed up changes over time. He observed that the 1960s – a period when young people broke with traditions, questioned sexual norms and demonstrated against political and educational institutions – was a time of strong 'intellectual ferment' too. Professions, until then accepted as involving expertise and altruism, started to be questioned. He explains:

> *Under the ideological influence of the period, historians and sociologists began producing 'revisionist' histories of the professions and their institutions, emphasizing their economic self-interest and concern for their status in the policies they pursued, and analyzing how their activities facilitated control of the poor, the working class and the deviant ... Influential sociological essays warned against adoption of the professions' own self-advertisements and, denying the possibility of neutrality, urged ... a more critical stance ... In the early 1970s, the primary target of most of the British and American writers was medicine – how it dominated social policy, the other occupations in the health-care division of labor, the institutions in which its members work, the patients or consumers, and how it has 'medicalized' personal and social problems.*

*(Freidson, 1994, pp. 3–4)*

Freidson identifies a further shift, starting towards the end of the 1970s, when sociologists started predicting a decline in the power of the professions. They then traced the way state policies were starting to challenge professions to produce evidence for the efficiency and effectiveness of their practices and to show that they were more accountable for their actions. How are we to assess this?

To begin, let us go back to the more traditional idea of defining professions as special and different. Gomm has provided a useful six-point summary of what are frequently said to be the key features or defining traits of professions.

> *Professions are occupations:*
> - *that have a philosophy of public service and altruism*
> - *that have skills based on theoretical knowledge derived from research*
> - *where members receive an extensive period of education and training prior to practising*
> - *where members are tested for their competence before being allowed to practise*
> - *where there is an explicit code of conduct for practice*
> - *where the occupational group is allowed to regulate itself.*
>
> *(Gomm, 1996, p. 115)*

---

### Activity 13    Professions in health and social care

*Allow about 15 minutes*    Taking this list of defining features, which of the following would you regard as professions?
- nurses
- social workers
- midwives
- occupational therapists.

Does the result fit with your own view?

---

Comment    If you had difficulty in deciding, you would not be alone. Measured against a list of traits like this, all of these occupations at first seem to shape up well. Members of all of these groups are strongly committed to their work, they have had a lengthy educational preparation involving – unlike VQs – extensive theoretical work in the classroom as well as practice. Yet are they comparable in these respects to medicine or the law? Thinking back to the census classification which was discussed early on in this unit, social workers were allocated to the professions category, but others were associate professional occupations.

Gomm comments that lists like this do capture something of the everyday meaning of profession, but 'they always founder on the issue of how much of each characteristic an occupation has to have before it can be called a profession' (p. 115). He points out that Freidson's more sceptical approach offers a way out. We should not think of this list of traits as *defining features* of professions. Instead they should be seen as *claims* made by groups aspiring to be considered as professions. Some groups have been more successful than others in getting their claims upheld.

Gomm then provides us with a second list which looks at professions as occupations which have successfully claimed control over their own work.

> *Professions can:*
>
> - *monopolise certain areas of work as their own*
> - *prohibit others from doing that work*
> - *make impersonating a member of the profession a criminal offence*
> - *define for themselves and others how the work ought to be performed*
> - *select new entrants*
> - *define the curriculum and assessment for training*
> - *set and police codes of conduct for practice and discipline.*
>
> *(Gomm, 1996, p. 116)*

The picture now starts to reflect the anti-professional comments of the course testers I quoted earlier. Is it necessary that professions have the degree of autonomy represented by this list? Should they define the work, select new entrants and exercise all the other controls set out here? The professions' own answers would be yes – they would say that others do not understand the issues and that professions can be trusted to regulate themselves and act in the interests of us all. We need to dig a little deeper and try to assess what has been called 'professional self-regulation'. (You have already met a brief discussion of this theme in Unit 24, where different kinds of accountability, including professional accountability, were discussed.)

## 4.2 The question of professional self-regulation

Of all the professions in the health and social care field, medicine is the one that started earliest and has travelled furthest along the road to self-regulation. The 1858 Medical Act first gave the profession a body, set up by statute and comprised overwhelmingly of doctors, with the power to keep a register of practitioners. That body, the General Medical Council (GMC) decides what qualifications are necessary for someone's name to be entered on the register and also investigates cases of misconduct that warrant removal from the register. Unless a doctor has been through a recognised training and his or her name is on the register, he or she is not entitled in law to practise medicine. All appointments as doctors in the NHS are appointments of registered practitioners. The GMC issues guidance to educational establishments on the curriculum. It provides a code of conduct to which doctors are expected to adhere and which can be used against them in cases of misconduct. It arranges to hear cases of misconduct and can strike doctors off the register – thus leaving them without the possibility of practising their profession. The GMC is also regularly consulted by governments about changes in health care policy.

 Other occupational groups in the health care field gained professional status in the sense of the right to maintain a register early in the twentieth century – among them midwifery (1902), nursing (1919) and dentistry (1921). The Council for Professions Supplementary to Medicine was set up in 1960 and covered what are increasingly today called allied health professions – for example, chiropody, dietetics, medical laboratory science, orthoptics, physiotherapy and radiography. Nurses, midwives and health visitors were brought together under a single UK Central Council in 1979 (UKCC). A General Osteopathic Council was set up in 1993 broadly on the model of the GMC. Until very recently, the social care field – while the Central Council for Education and Training in Social Work regulated social work educational programmes – did not have a full-scale regulatory function and a statutory register. But things have changed, as the box below shows.

---

**Developments in the regulation of the professions**

April 2002 saw the start of two new bodies. The Health Professions Council replaced the CPSM and the Nursing and Midwifery Council replaced the United Kingdom Central Council for Nursing, Midwifery and Health Visiting (UKCC). Both are much smaller than the previous bodies and they have a bigger proportion of Council members from outside the professions. The GMC, after much discussion, seemed set to go in a similar direction.

There were important developments in the social care sector too. The General Social Care Council for England began work as a regulatory body with powers to register care workers at around the same time. The GSCC plan – in contrast with the health sector – was to include everyone from the start and to work to set standards and ensure that over time people were enabled to meet them. And instead of a code of conduct just for social workers, one of its first actions was to consult widely on codes for all social care workers and their employers (see Unit 3).

What was the significance of all this? Redesigning the health regulatory bodies, we could say, was starting to take the 'self' out of self-regulation. And the GSCC, in some ways turned regulation upside down – since instead of excluding people without the right educational preparation, it included everyone with a view to progressively improving their standards of education and training.

Want to know more? Websites for the new bodies mentioned here are:

www.gscc.org.uk [accessed 5.8.02]

www.nmc-uk.org [accessed 5.8.02]

www.hpcuk.org [accessed 5.8.02]

When I looked in May 2002, there was also a website for the Northern Ireland Social Care Council www.dhsspsni.gov.uk/hss/niscc. The website for the Care Council for Wales was under construction www.ccwales.org.uk. Details about the Scottish Social Services Council were to be found on www.sssc.uk.com [accessed 24.9.02]

Addresses for contacting these bodies can be found in *Getting a Vocational Qualification: A K100 Student's Guide.*

---

Why has there been so much sudden change? To answer this we need to step back a little and ask what regulation of professions is about – and why old-style self-regulation is no longer as acceptable as it once was.

The powers to register practitioners that professions gained historically put them in a privileged and protected place – defining who could join their ranks, what preparation they must receive and what was to be done if a practising professional fell below the expected standards. Parliament granted these powers of self-regulation and judged them to be in the interests of the public. A government enquiry into the medical profession in the 1970s endorsed this and suggested that we see self-regulation as:

> *... a contract between public and profession, by which the public go to the profession for medical treatment because the profession has made sure it will provide satisfactory treatment.*

> *(Merrison, 1975, p. 3)*

---

Activity 14  **Trusting the professionals**

*Allow about 15 minutes*  Is it in the best interests of the public that the various health care professions regulate themselves in this way? Try to set out what this system can offer if it is working well and what the dangers are if it does not work well.

---

Comment  If it is working well, self-regulation ensures for the public:

- that all practitioners are trained to give a *common standard* of care; that they are strongly *committed* to their work and are aware of ethical issues; that they are *up to date* in their practice; that *knowledge is being improved* and developed at all times; that there is an *effective route of complaint* if things go wrong.

If it is not working well:

- members of the profession can become overly *protective* of each other and of their work; they can *restrict access* to training; they can *fail to adjust boundaries* with co-workers and work in teams effectively; they can *ignore the importance of a lay input*; the education they provide can become *inward-looking and out of touch* with the needs of people.

In recent years, there has been a growing concern that professional self-regulation is not working well enough. The GMC and the doctors, in particular have come under heavy fire. A series of cases of poor practice, misconduct and sometimes criminal behaviour have hit the headlines. Here are some of the ones that gained most public attention.

- *The Bristol doctors case* This concerned complicated heart surgery on babies and young children at Bristol Royal Infirmary. Doctors ignored warnings from colleagues that performance in their operations was below the national average and that their death rates were unacceptably high. Consultant surgeon James Wisheart was struck off the register; consultant surgeon Janaradan Dhasmana was banned for three years from operating on children. Dr John Roylance, who was Chief Executive at the hospital at the time, was found to have ignored warnings from other doctors about the performance of these surgeons and was also struck off the register. This was the longest ever case heard by the GMC. It opened in October 1997, and decisions were made public the following June. At that point the government announced a public inquiry, chaired by Ian Kennedy, QC. The inquiry examined the circumstances at Bristol and moved on to examine wider issues of the running of the NHS more broadly. It also explored the issue of the retention without full parental consent of organs from children who died in hospital. The final report of the public inquiry was published in July 2001 (Secretary of State for Health, 2001) and the government issued a formal response to its 198 recommendations the following January.

- *The Shipman case* Dr Harold Shipman, a Greater Manchester GP, was found guilty in the criminal courts in January 2000 of murdering 15 elderly female patients with injections of diamorphine. He was suspected of causing up to 160 further deaths. The case came to light after Shipman had attempted to forge a will. The press followed the case in detail and it remained headline news for a considerable period after the conviction. Again a public inquiry was announced. It was charged with exploring all the agencies involved and making recommendations about changes in procedure to prevent a GP's behaviour not being effectively challenged for such a long period. The decision of the GMC 24 years earlier not to strike Shipman's name from the register following a conviction for forging prescriptions and for drug offences was also called into question.

- *The Ledward case* Ten complaints against Rodney Ledward, a gynaecologist who had worked in NHS and private hospitals in Kent, were upheld by the GMC in 1998 and led to his removal from the register. The publicity resulted in a stream of further patients coming forward, uncovering a catalogue of incompetent surgery and belittling of patients which had apparently gone unchallenged over many years. His flamboyant and arrogant style and his refusal to accept that he was anything but a first class surgeon horrified and dismayed colleagues and public alike. A public inquiry chaired by Jean Ritchie QC damned him for his arrogance, lack of compassion and his intimidating style. The story continued to run as the Royal Pharmaceutical Society of Great Britain initiated an inquiry on account of his alleged practice as a pharmacist in Ireland and later, as reports of his death were announced then cast into doubt.

With these and other stories repeatedly in the headlines, it looked to the press, the public and the politicians, as if the professions could not be trusted to regulate themselves in the interests of the public.

Should we abandon professional self-regulation in the face of all this criticism?

Reg Pyne – for many years the UKCC officer responsible for professional conduct and disciplinary cases in nursing, midwifery and health visiting – is an interesting case. His classic textbook on how the business of removal from the register works was first issued in 1981. In the first edition and the second edition, he argued, following the Merrison line, that accepting the responsibility to regulate itself and to do this in the interests of the public was the hallmark of a profession. His passionate belief in self-regulation was very clear. But in 1998, he changed tack.

*Parents at the GMC hearing demonstrated against the Bristol doctors. Other parents, as the public inquiry opened, demonstrated in support of them*

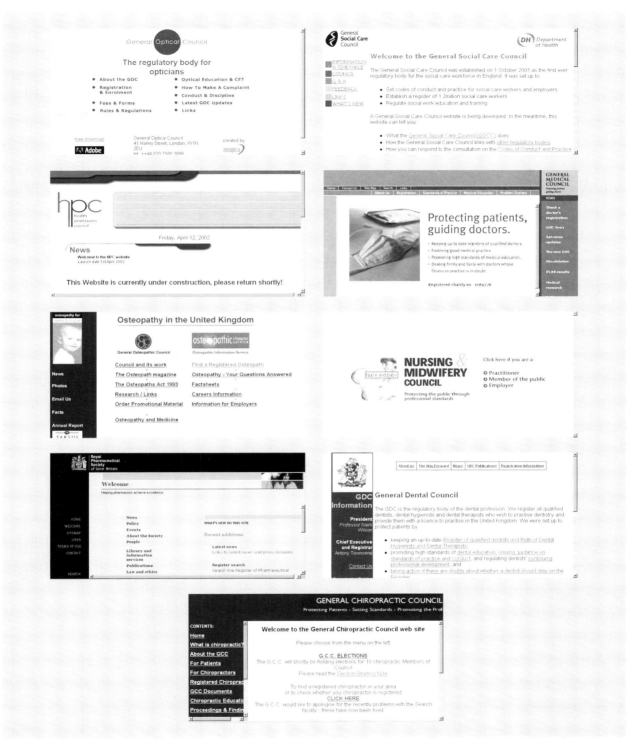

*All the regulatory bodies have websites designed to give information to the public and the profession. Here are some of them as they appeared in Spring 2002*

He argued that the professions must become much more active and open about their regulatory work. They must let people know, for example, of the measures they are taking to ensure practitioners keep up to date. They must publicise cases where professionals are *not* removed from the register rather than leaving the media to cover only the more lurid cases involving people being struck off for criminal conduct or sexual improprieties. They should also be letting the wider public know of those cases where, although individuals have come before a disciplinary hearing, the real issue is insufficient management support or not enough staff for them to carry out their job properly.

Why this change? Having retired from the UKCC in 1995, Reg Pyne had begun to see things through different eyes. He became actively involved in health issues in his local area and strongly involved with local health consumer groups. He could see just how little ordinary people knew and understood about what the regulatory body did and why. If there was more information, he reasoned, people might see the positive side of regulation and not just the cases where things had gone very wrong (Pyne, 1998, pp. 96-102). He was writing just before the Bristol doctors scandal broke, but he was already saying that regulatory bodies had to take a hard look at themselves and at the confidence gap that was opening up between them and the public.

Patient groups and health service consumer organisations, by now, were also starting to look into regulation – raising questions about the whole system of self-regulation and how it fitted together (see box). Among the things they recommended were much clearer standards, good publicity, substantial representation and clear balancing of consumer, lay and other interests on the bodies as well as strong external consultation with all relevant stakeholders.

---

**Outsiders start to look at professional self-regulation**

The National Consumer Council recognised the growing public concern about high profile cases of professional misconduct and commissioned a report. Here are some of the questions it raised:

- Why do bodies have different powers to sanction professionals, different ways of doing things and different composition and memberships?

- Why are some groups statutorily regulated and others not?

- How do the different ways of dealing with problems and complaints at local level and through regulatory bodies join up?

- How do consumers find out about standards and what checks can they make?

- Is there not a conflict of interest when some bodies have a dual role of promoting and regulating the profession?

The NCC commented:

'... we found a patchwork of varying arrangements for different professions ... which has not caught up with changes in public demand or with current health practices.' (p1)

*(Adapted from NCC, 1999)*

---

An overarching body, the Council for the Regulation of Health Professions, was set to come into being in 2003, with the aim of encouraging more sharing of good practice across the health regulatory bodies. Even before it started, some people were saying it was not enough. User-friendliness, they said, meant going for one single regulatory body across health and social care with a clear lay majority. It was an idea, not surprisingly, that made the professionals nervous.

Activity 15

Allow about 15 minutes

## User-friendly professional regulation?

Offprint 34 is an excerpt from an interview with Lynne Berry, the Chief Executive of the new regulatory body for workers in social care in England – the General Social Care Council (GSCC). While regulatory body reform in health is a difficult matter with eight bodies already established and in different stages of change – the GSCC is starting with a clean slate. How far do you think it is going to meet the concerns of service users? (The article gives you a lot of information about the care sector and about the activities and timetable of the GSCC. But it is the comments of Lynne Berry herself that give more direct clues.)

Comment

I found three things on the plus side. Lynne Berry firmly puts the public first. Notice how she talks of what the public has a right to expect. Next, she emphasises that the council is going to use clear and simple language about what we the public can expect of a care worker. People on the register will have to subscribe to standards as set out in a code (see Unit 3) and can be removed for breaching it. Third, the GSCC is going to cover all care workers, making things easier to understand. Fourth, it will have a lay majority. She makes a real point of saying that it is not the 'closed club' of self-regulation, but that it is regulation by people who use services as well as experts in the professional field.

You may have expressed worries too. The system looks set to be complex with a raft of new agencies at local and national level. There is no mention, for example, of whether the devolved administrations will set different standards. And you might well be thinking that 'the devil is in the detail'. Set entry standards too high and it will look like old-style regulation – leaving people outside the system giving unregulated care. Set standards too low and will they mean anything? And how will Lynne and her colleagues ensure that all voices are heard? Finally, what happens when care teams are drawn, as they so often are, from across health and social care? The chances are that a complainant will get lost in a regulatory maze.

To sum up: there are clear moves now away from professional *self-*regulation in social care and in health. Whether these moves will amount to genuine *co-*regulation, with all interested parties helping to shape standards, remains to be seen.

## 4.3 Towards a new model of professionalism?

Maybe we need more than adjustments to structures for professional regulation. Perhaps we need a new kind of professional person, who is more open and sharing of expertise and who leaves more room in their day-to-day practice for lay people and colleagues to have a say.

Activity 16

Allow about 30 minutes

## What would a new professional look like?

Read Chapter 22 in the Reader. This chapter argues that there is an important sense in which the idea of profession is based on an outdated notion of professional work which overplays the importance of formal scientific knowledge. It also argues that outdated images of masculinity and femininity underpin it.

(a) What are the key features proposed in the chapter for new professionalism?

(b)    Is the argument that these are a feminine way of being professional?

(c)    Do you consider that new professionalism offers a more useful way of thinking about caring work than old professionalism?

Comment    (a)    Key features of 'new professionalism' are summarised in the right-hand column of the table in the chapter (p. 193). They involve: a less elitist attitude to 'mastery' of knowledge; a recognition that members of the care team really are a team and one that includes the patient; taking collective responsibility; providing support to practitioners; and an abandonment of the mask of detachment in favour of recognising that practitioners' personal attributes, like age and sex, might have a bearing on successful intervention. In short, this means a model that creates more equality between the service giver and service user rather than one portraying the one party as a fount of all wisdom and the other as entirely without knowledge and skill.

(b)    No. The argument is that the rigid dichotomy between so-called masculine and feminine traits that is part of our inheritance needs to be overturned by new thinking which is not dependent on gender categories.

(c)    The model probably needs to be spelt out more for particular areas of work, but it does chime with contemporary values of partnership, user-centredness, respect for the client/patient, and so on.

All in all then, the question of professions in health and social care is a controversial one. Freidson, writing in the mid-1990s, wanted to see professions being more open about what they do. But he also wanted to be sure that bureaucratic rules and economic pressures do not work against the proper exercise of professional judgements. He wrote in terms of 'nourishing professionalism' by 'saving professionalism from itself'. And he warned:

> *Measures designed solely to counteract professional abuse without also strengthening professionalism itself will lead us to an impoverished, and maybe not even cost-controlled, health system that neither physicians nor patients deserve.*

> *(Freidson, 1994, p. 198)*

His view continues to be that we need strong and autonomous professionals, able to champion the cause of their expertise (Freidson, 2001, p.215). You may or may not agree. After the Bristol doctors case, one thing that the public inquiry called for was a broadened notion of competence for professionals. They should have relevant and up-to-date knowledge and skills, but non-clinical skills were equally important They should be educated in communication and teamworking. They should have an understanding of the principles and organisation of the NHS, and leadership should be a priority (Secretary of State for Health, 2001, chapter 25).

This section started with the difficulty of defining a profession. We saw that this was not just a matter of who should have a prestigious title, but of how care workers should be accountable and whether self-regulation was justified. From a user point of view, we need to be sure that work done in the name of care is of high quality – especially when many of those receiving it are vulnerable. But we also need to be sure that those who are working in care have access to the kind of training and support that will enable them to give of their best, without feeling they are constantly at risk of being reported (Annandale's concept of defensive practice is relevant here – see the Reader and Unit 24). While maintaining some aspect of the self-regulation which has been the defining feature of their work, professions need to acknowledge the criticisms others have made of them. What we need in particular, is new thinking about the gulf that there has been in the past between professional work and that of others, and a more clearly shared vision about how care workers of all kinds can work together better in the interests of their patients and clients.

---

**Key points**

- Professions can be defined as occupations that make strong claims to self-regulation on the basis of their knowledge and skill.

- Successful professions won considerable statutory power to run their own affairs, but this right to self-regulation has come under fire in recent years by government and by service user organisations.

- Rigid distinctions among professions and between professions and other groups of workers are not always in the best interests of the public as service users.

- Professional self-regulation is in process of being reformed. Whether the new arrangements will serve the public interest more clearly remains to be seen.

# Section 5
# Care qualifications – vocational, professional, or both?

It is time to return to the question of vocational qualifications. How do the two structures – VQs and professional qualifications – fit together? Should a boundary between the two remain, or should professions and VQs be merged? Many now agree that in the early days of the VQ system the pendulum swung too far towards employers' needs for practical skills and too far away from the knowledge base in professional education. In the eyes of people developing VQs, the professions, and especially the educational segments of the professions, looked too remote from the real world of employment. As a result, employers had the lead and the professions – whether by choice or design – were not closely involved. In return, the professions were often witheringly critical of the VQ system. VQs, they said, produced robots, people who could only follow rules, people who knew 'how' but did not know 'why'! In this atmosphere of mutual criticism there was little incentive to work together. Is thinking so polarised today?

---

Activity 17 **Poles apart?**

*Allow about 10 minutes*

Below is a list of criteria we might use to evaluate the strengths and weaknesses of vocational qualifications versus professional ones. See if you can put a tick or cross beside each to show whether they are strong or weak in relation to each one. Do not spend a lot of time on this – just work from your thinking now.

|                                          | VQ | PQ |
|------------------------------------------|----|----|
| (a) Provides open access                 |    |    |
| (b) Gives strong guarantee of standard   |    |    |
| (c) Offers flexibility                   |    |    |
| (d) Facilitates updating                 |    |    |
| (e) Strong employment relevance          |    |    |
| (f) Gives depth of knowledge             |    |    |
| (g) Inculcates ethical perspectives      |    |    |
| (h) Offers a clear and simple framework  |    |    |

---

Comment

As a rough and ready summary, I thought that (a), (c) and (e) comparatively speaking were the strengths of the VQ system and (b), (d) and (f) were the strengths of professional qualifications. I thought that (g) was a feature of both, although professional preparations clearly provided much greater depth on this. Finally, I thought that neither could be counted as strong on criterion (h), so I put a cross in both columns. Your judgements, however, might well differ on some of these items. You might have found yourself saying, 'it depends how they are developed ...' or 'things are changing ...'. This was a view put strongly by some of our testers who were involved in VQ work in the mid-1990s. Even mentioning these differences, some of them felt, perpetuated old debates.

So how do things look now? Have these two systems been fully integrated? Over the last few years, there has been more and more coming together. Take social work. In 1992, the CCETSW, the body then responsible for education and training, began to work with the competency idea. The result was the Diploma in Social Work qualification. It placed six named areas of competence – statements not of what knowledge a social worker must have, but of what a social worker must be able to do – at its heart (CCETSW, 1995).

Critics at the time argued that the VQ-type system, strongly influenced by employers and focusing on their immediate needs, threatened to destroy the independence of social work professionals and the wider role that they can play as advocates for their clients and constructive critics of policy development (Dominelli, 1996). Government recognised the force of these arguments but it remained determined to develop VQ thinking at higher levels and to move preparation for the professions in this direction (DfEE, 1996). From 2003, social worker entry will be via a three-year degree programme rather than the two-year diploma. This new programme, while certainly emphasising theory, remains strongly influenced by practical skills and competence thinking. National occupational standards, detailing what a newly qualified practitioner should be competent to do, will be an integral part of the qualification.

## Back to the bedpans for student nurses

Ian Murray, medical correspondent

FRANK DOBSON is planning to turn back the clock and take training for nurses out of the classroom and put it back into hospitals.

In an attempt to recruit the numbers needed to make good the chronic nursing shortage, the Health Secretary is determined to reintroduce a more practical training course. He believes that 1980s reforms which made training more academic, with universities running courses instead of hospitals, have backfired.

(*The Times* (London) January 16, 1999, Saturday)

The health professions, so far at least, have not gone the same route. The statutory regulatory bodies have retained decision-making power about the standards to meet at registration. There has not been a framework of national occupational standards in the same way as in social work. Nursing education is an interesting case. In the early 1990s, it moved more towards the academic end, shifting into the university setting and giving a Diploma in Higher Education at the point of registration. But tensions soon emerged. Newspapers campaigned for a more practical nurse. An influential government report criticised all the health professions for elitist attitudes and 'academic drift' and argued that the NHS, paying for education, should shape it more directly (Department of Health, 2000a). Could these students do several things at once? Could they end up:

- *'fit for award'* (meeting the academic standards of a diploma or degree)

- *'fit for practice'* (meeting the requirements of the professional body of someone able to act as a professional and to develop)

- and *'fit for purpose'* (able to get out there on day one and do the job as the employers wanted)?

Government had this last fitness in mind. It wanted more flexible career pathways into and within the profession, with, for example, cadet schemes, fast track entry for health care assistants, more stepping on and stepping off points (Department of Health, 1999). Pilot schemes quickly got under way.

The publication of the NHS Plan (Department of Health, 2000b) signalled even more fundamental reform of education in the health area, promising funding for programmes of shared learning across the health professions as a way of breaking down the rigid boundaries the professions had built up and individual NHS learning accounts to get people onto an educational ladder. Things began to develop. Reforms to pay and grading and terms of conditions were accompanied by a framework for lifelong learning (see box). Underpinning it was a belief that if the NHS were to improve, *all* staff needed better access to education and training opportunities. There was talk of a 'skills' escalator' for those at the bottom and something like a climbing frame so that those in one professional area might be able to move diagonally across rather than remaining in single professional silos or going to the bottom and starting again. It would be a brave new world indeed if these arrangements, as one press commentator put it, really meant a future where porters could become consultants (The Times, 22 May 2001).

---

**Learning for everyone in the NHS**

The new framework for lifelong learning announced in 2001 includes:

- A common induction programme for everyone

- A 'skills escalator' for those without professional qualifications, giving them NHS Learning Accounts and personal development plans, enabling them to obtain basic skills and NVQs and to progress into new roles

- Common principles and shared learning for all pre-registration education – to be in place for all by 2004

- Continuing professional development and new approaches to leadership, all involving work-based and multi-disciplinary learning

- More investment in mentoring and supervising roles - taking learning to people when and where they need it

- An NHS University to support all staff in developing their learning

*(Department of Health, 2001)*

---

Meanwhile, the vocational qualifications system as a whole has also been coming together more. There has been a shake-up in school-based VQs (GNVQs) and in the Modern Apprenticeships Scheme for young people. There is now a network of opportunities provided through

LearnDirect and Learning and Skills Councils for people to sign up for skills training locally and to get access to advice as to just how to get onto a lifelong learning ladder – whatever their field of work and interest. On the website of the Qualifications and Curriculum Authority (QCA) you will find the National Qualifications Framework - a map of how academic professional and vocational qualifications hang together for England, Wales and Northern Ireland. The Scottish Parliament's Lifelong Learning Committee, which consulted widely on its proposals early in 2002, was envisaging something similar – wanting to make life simpler for the learner, and recommending a one-stop shop for information and advice (Wojtas, 2002). Universities, with their tradition of independence, are not directly part of these new frameworks, but perhaps it is on the cards.

| Level of qualification | General | Vocationally-related | | Occupational |
|---|---|---|---|---|
| **5** | Higher-level qualifications | | | Level 5 NVQ |
| **4** | | | | Level 4 NVQ |
| **3**<br>advanced level | A level | Free-standing mathematics units level 3 | Vocational A level (Advanced GNVQ) | Level 3 NVQ |
| **2**<br>intermediate level | GCSE grade A*-C | Free-standing mathematics units level 2 | Intermediate GNVQ | Level 2 NVQ |
| **1**<br>foundation level | GCSE grade D-G | Free-standing mathematics units level 1 | Foundation GNVQ | Level 1 NVQ |
| Entry level | Certificate of (educational) achievement | | | |

 *The National Qualifications Framework: how the jigsaw fits together (Source: QCA website: www.qca.org.uk/ [accessed 7.4.02])*

Where have user voices been in all this debate about more training and better standards? In the VQ world, consultation and respect for user choices are values that are promoted. Direct user testimony about a candidate's performance can also be used as evidence for an award. Educators in the professions too are realising that students need to be exposed directly to service users and patients. They are bringing patients into the lecture hall and sending students out into the community to see the conditions in which people live. It is still too early to judge whether user voices on the new regulatory bodies examined in Section 4 will be powerful.

Education and training for members of the public who increasingly sit on bodies concerned with health and social care is likely to rise up the agenda in coming years. The College of Health, a body dedicated to creating more patient-focused care, recommends new training should be designed to enable a wide range of people to get their voices heard. Sometimes what is needed is *joint* training for health professionals and lay representatives if we are going to enable real dialogue to take place (College of Health, 1999).

In this busy world of reorganisation and policy change in education and training, however, one thing stands out. There are still multiple agencies and multiple interest groups involved. Government is intervening to try to reshape the workforce and create more flexibility in how care is delivered. Professional bodies still argue that they each need to have a major say in standards for education. Universities tend to protect their autonomy and the Sector Skills Councils (the old NTOs) – building the VQ system – have a more powerful voice in some sectors than in others. The result is a confusion of standards with overlaps and gaps. People rightly argue that change is under way. But it does still seem that those at the bottom of the system find it hard to get their skills recognised, rewarded and developed, that those at the top remain defensive about their territory, and those in the middle find it hard to forge new pathways for themselves.

---

**Key points**

- There has been a history of tension between professional and vocational qualifications, although the two have been coming closer together in recent years.

- Government has been criticising the professions and putting funding behind new routes and pathways through training with the aim of creating lifelong learning and a more flexible and responsive workforce.

- The many interest groups that are involved, the complexity of the system and the repeated changes to it have all worked against creating the simplicity and clarity that many say they would like to achieve.

# Conclusion

This unit has been concerned with all those people who carry out the work of caring for others and in particular with their education and training. We have seen that unpaid and untrained carers outnumber those who are paid and formally prepared for caring work. We have also seen that paid care work is contained in a complex array of separate and hierarchically arranged occupations and professions whose work in practice overlaps. Furthermore, because care work is often done by women and straddles the public world of work and the private world of home, the skills that are involved in caring have tended to be undervalued and overlooked. Vocational qualifications in care offer an approach where caring skills have begun to be named and workers recognised in new ways. This sits uneasily, however, alongside a long history of separation and self-regulation in the health care professions, and separation between health and social care.

The title of this unit asks whether the overall system of qualifications in caring is a pattern or a patchwork. Opportunities to get training in care work and to find pathways of development across and between areas in a more flexible way than before, are undoubtedly growing. Whether we have arrived at that simple, coherent unified system that was the vision nearly 20 years ago when VQs first started is more questionable. 'Not yet', would be my answer. There are still too many invisible contributors to care, too many different bodies involved, with too much overlap and tension between them. There is a way to go before we can say there is more of a pattern than a patchwork.

---

**Study skills:   The psychology of exams**

Up to now you've focused mainly on getting yourself sorted out for revision. But it's also worth thinking ahead about how to gear yourself up for the exam. You may not be able to think so calmly about it when the time comes. It's really a matter of analysing carefully what you are hoping to achieve. Let's assume that you aren't going to be struck by a sudden, lucky inspiration in the exam room, and that you'll just have to rely on what an ordinary mind and body can achieve in three hours. How can you give yourself the best chance of a peak performance? You can get some ideas by reading Section 5 of Chapter 7 of *The Good Study Guide* now.

When you have read it, take careful note that you don't want to be doing a lot of deep or creative *thinking* in an exam. You want to spend as high a proportion of the time as you can writing fluently, responding to the point of the questions. The aim is to reveal as much as possible of your knowledge and understanding of the course. This means that you need to:

- get your knowledge of the course 'boiled down' into condensed, well-structured notes, so that it's quickly accessible at a moment's notice

- keep practising with exam-type questions until you have a slick technique for picking out key words and sketching out a plan

- be very clear about the three-part structure of the paper and which questions you have prepared yourself to answer

- be disciplined in your use of time in the exam.

Perhaps you feel guilty about not having studied every part of the course in detail, in which case you might think it's the thoroughness of your revision that is going to count for most in the exam. Or if you lack confidence in your understanding of the course, you might imagine that it's the profound originality of answers that brings success. However, the truth is much more prosaic. It's being realistic, well organised, well practised and tightly planned that produces a peak performance. These are things you can still achieve if you make the time.

# References

Arber, S. and Ginn, J. (1990) 'The meaning of informal care: gender and the contribution of elderly people', *Ageing and Society*, Vol. 10, No. 4, pp. 429–54.

Bibbings, A. (1994) 'Carers and Professionals – the Carer's Viewpoint', in A Leathard (ed) *Going Inter-Professional*, Routledge, London.

Bytheway, B. and Johnson, J. (1998) 'The social construction of carers' in Symonds, A. and Kelly, A. (eds) *The Social Construction of Care in the Community*, Macmillan, London.

College of Health (1999) *Voices in Action*, Department of Health/College of Heath, London.

Central Council for Education and Training in Social Work (1995) *Assuring Quality in the Diploma in Social Work – (1) : Rules and Requirements for the DipSW*, CCETSW (2nd edn), London.

Davies, C. and Rosser, J. (1987) 'What would we do without her?: invisible women in NHS administration', in Spencer, A. and Podmore, D. (eds) *In a Man's World: Essays on Women in Male-Dominated Professions*, Tavistock, London.

Department for Education and Employment (1996) *Higher Level Vocational Qualifications – A Government Position Paper*, DfEE, Sheffield.

Department of Health (1999) *Making a Difference: Strengthening the nursing, midwifery and health visiting contribution to health and healthcare*, Department of Health, London.

Department of Health (2000a) *A Health Service of All the Talents: developing the NHS Workforce. Consultation document.* Department of Health, London. www.doh.gov.uk/wfprconsult/index.htm [accessed: 24.9.02]

Department of Health (2000b) *The NHS Plan a plan for investment. A plan for reform*, (Cm 4818-1). The Stationery Office, London. www.nhs.uk/nationalplan/ [accessed: 24.9.02]

Department of Health (2001) *'Working Together- Learning Together': a framework for lifelong learning for the NHS*, Department of Health, London. www.doh.gov.uk/lifelonglearning/index.htm [accessed: 24.9.02]

Dominelli, L. (1996) 'Deprofessionalizing social work: anti-oppressive practice, competencies and postmodernism', *The British Journal of Social Work*, Vol. 26, No. 2, pp. 153–75.

Dunlop, M. (1996) NVQs in care – how 'national' are they?, *Association of Social Care Trainers Newsletter*, Vol. 29, October, pp. 12–14.

Eraut, M., Steadman, S., Trill, J. and Parker, J. (1996) *The Assessment of NVQs*, University of Sussex, Institute of Education, Brighton.

Freidson, E. (1994) *Professionalism Reborn*, Polity Press, Oxford.

Freidson, E (2001) *Professionalism: the third logic*, Polity Press, Cambridge.

Gomm, R. (l996) 'Professions and professionalism' in Aitkin, V. and Jellico, H. (eds) *Behavioural Sciences for Health Professionals*, W.B. Saunders, London.

Merrison, A. (1975) *Report of the Committee of Inquiry into the Regulation of the Medical Profession* (Cmnd 6018), HMSO, London.

National Consumer Council (1999) *Self-regulation of Professionals in Health Care: consumer issues*, NCC, London.

National Council for Vocational Qualifications, *Annual Report 1993–4*, NCVQ, London.

National Statistics website www.statistics.gov.uk/census2001/default. asp [accessed: 21.2.02]

OPCS (1994) *Census 1991, Economic Activity, Great Britain, Vol. 2*, HMSO, London.

Parker, G. (1992) 'Counting care: numbers and types of informal carers' in Twigg, J. (ed.) *Carers: Research and Practice*, HMSO, London.

Pyne, R (1998) *Professional Discipline in Nursing, Midwifery and Health Visiting*, 3rd edn, Blackwell, Oxford.

QCA website www.qca.org.uk [accessed: 7.4.02]

Redding, D. (1991) 'Exploding the myth', *Community Care*, 12 December, pp. 18–20.

Secretary of State for Health (2001) *Learning from Bristol: The report of the public inquiry into children's heart surgery at the Bristol Royal Infirmary 1984–1995*, (CM 5207(1). The Stationery Office, London. (Kennedy Report)

South Australian Department of Labour, Women's Adviser's Unit (1992) *A Window on Women's Skills in Administrative and Clerical Work. Practical Guide*, South Australian Department of Labour, Adelaide, South Australia.

Taylor, M. (1995) 'Voluntary action and the state' in Gladstone, D. (ed.) *British Social Welfare: Past, Present and Future*, UCL Press, London.

Thornley, C (1997) *The invisible workers: an investigation into the pay and employment of healthcare assistants in the NHS*, Unison, London.

Thornley, C. (2001) *Non-Registered Nurses in the NHS – an update*, Unison, London.

Toye, J. and Vigor, P. (1994) *Implementing NVQs: The Experience of Employers, Employees and Trainees*, Report No. 265, Institute of Manpower Studies, Brighton.

Wojtas, O. (2002) 'Smarter Way for a Nation to Learn', *Times Higher Education Supplement*, 29 March.

# Acknowledgements

Grateful acknowledgement is made to the following sources for permission to reproduce material in this unit:

## Text

*p. 11:* Census 2001 (England Household Form) Specimen. Crown Copyright material is reproduced under Class Licence Number COIW0000065 with the permission of the Controller of HMSO and the Queen's Printer for Scotland.

## Tables

*p. 59:* QCA-National Qualifications Framework website page: www.qca.or.uk/nq/framework, Copyright © Qualifications and Curriculum Authority.

## Illustrations

*p. 10 and 17:* Maggie Guillon; *p. 50, top:* The Times N I Syndication; *p. 50, bottom:* The Press Association Limited, 2001; *p. 51, top left:* General Optical Council; *p. 51, top right:* General Social Care Council; *p. 51, second left:* The General Optical Council; *p. 51, second right:* General Medical Council; *p. 51, third left:* General Osteopathic Council; *p. 51, third right:* Nursing and Midwifery Council; *p. 51, fourth left:* Royal Pharmaceutical Society of Great Britain; *p. 51, fourth right:* General Dental Council; *p. 51, bottom:* General Chiropractic Council.

Every effort has been made to contact copyright holders. If any have been inadvertently overlooked the publishers will be pleased to make the necessary arrangements at the first opportunity.

# Unit 27
# Care Policies and Care Politics

Prepared for the course team by Celia Davies

Updated by the author

While you are working on Unit 27, you will need:

- Course Reader
- Offprints Book
- *The Good Study Guide*
- Care Systems and Structures
- Wallchart

# Contents

# Introduction

This unit will examine the thinking behind provision of services for health and social care. Have the amount and kinds of public provision changed? If so, when and why? How, as a society, have we thought about what the state should do and what we should do for ourselves? What should we be paying for? What should we be doing voluntarily in support of others? Back in the 1980s there was a strong argument that the welfare state had lost direction. The Conservative governments of the time argued that limited resources had to be targeted at those in real need, that there should be more market competition and more consumer choice. Labour, elected in 1997, took things in a rather different direction. Debates, however, continue to rage about what is to be done with public services, and how they are to be organised.

---

**Core questions**

- What are the underlying ideas which prompt state provision of health and social care?

- Who influences the direction care services are taking?

- Do services respond to user needs and offer real choices?

- Has sufficient priority been given to groups who are likely to be neglected?

---

Questions like these can be highly controversial ones and involve party politics. It is not the aim of this unit to take a political stance. Instead it will examine the arguments and the implications of decisions that have been taken at different times. Having reached this point in the course, you already have the resources to answer many of the questions tackled in this unit. You may well be pleasantly surprised at the links you can make.

# Section 1

# Who supports the welfare state?

Today's health and welfare provisions are part of what has come to be known as the welfare state, a set of measures devised half a century ago to tackle poverty, and to provide education and housing, as well as health and social services. Services were to be provided mainly on the basis of need, funded largely from taxation and provided by public employees in state-owned and managed services. This vision of the welfare state, as you will see, was born in the inter-war years and given impetus by the experience of wartime. It was developed as a result of a landslide victory for the Labour Party in 1945 and had widespread public support. We will examine the ideas that underpinned the creation of the post-war welfare state in Section 2, some of its key developments in Section 3, and the recent challenges to it in Section 4. But to make a start, let us consider just what public support there is for health and social services now.

Activity 1 **Policy priorities**

*Allow about 15 minutes*
Not everyone agrees how far the state has a duty to intervene to support aspects of the lives of its citizens. Below are nine areas where you might feel that governments should or should not use public resources (taxpayers' money) to intervene. Note down beside each one of these roughly what percentage of people you think would agree that the government should carry out the responsibilities on the list. So, for example, if you think about half the people in a survey would say that the government should provide a job for everyone who wants one, put 50 per cent beside that item and so on through the list.

- Provide health care for the sick ............
- Provide a decent standard of living for the old ............
- Provide industry with the help it needs to grow............
- Give financial help to university students from low-income families ............
- Provide decent housing for those who can't afford it ............
- Keep prices under control ............
- Provide a decent standard of living for the unemployed ............
- Reduce income differences between the rich and the poor ............
- Provide a job for everyone who wants one ............

Comment
What you have been considering is a list that has been used in successive versions of the Social Attitudes Survey (a regular nation-wide survey consulting a sample of around 3,500 people in Great Britain, a separate survey being carried out for Northern Ireland). This part of the survey, which ran throughout the late 1980s, gauged the level of public support for certain forms of welfare spending and how far this has been changing. Unfortunately, questions were not asked and reported in exactly the same form in more recent years, so the 1990 results are the last ones that can be fully matched with your estimates. These results show high levels of support for every one of the measures on this list. There was strongest agreement that the state should be responsible for providing health care. It came top, with an overwhelming 98 per cent of those participating in the Social Attitudes Survey saying that this should either definitely or probably

be a government responsibility. Ninety per cent or more of people agreed with the next four items. The percentages then reduce as we go down the list, although still way over half, 60 per cent, said that providing a job for everyone was the government's responsibility (Taylor-Gooby, 1991).

Some political and academic commentators expressed surprise and disbelief at these findings. The responses were interpreted as no more than a wish-list – people *say* that the government should do these things, but they would not be prepared to see their own taxes go up. These sceptics also suggested that it was only the poor who wanted state services and that the rich, who can opt out, would not be prepared to subsidise others in this way.

The survey results, however, showed that willingness in principle to raise taxes to spend on these services actually increased in the course of the 1980s. Also, while, as you might expect, there was more support for these measures among Labour and Liberal Democrat supporters than among Conservatives, the rich emerged as stronger in their support for these measures and actually more prepared to support tax increases than are the poor (Taylor-Gooby, 1991). In 1999, two years after Labour had come to power and while it was still being cautious and holding down taxes, the British Social Attitudes Survey was again suggesting that the public would support more spending – especially on health and education (Hills and Lelkes, 1999). And in 2002, when Labour's budget included an equivalent of an extra 3p in the pound to pay for a doubled spend on the NHS over a decade, an opinion poll suggested that there was still considerable public support (Travis, 2002). To understand this strong support for public spending and public services, we need to go back to the origins of the welfare state, the vision which produced it and the way this vision captured imaginations and created loyalties – particularly to the NHS. You will see in this unit that important ideas about citizenship entitlements, morality and self-worth underpinned the new welfare state measures of the post-war period. The unit will also bring out some ideas – not discussed at the time – about what caring was and who should do it.

**Study skills:   Using the wallchart**

This is the unit where the wallchart 'A Century of Care Policy' comes into its own. If you have not been marking off items as they have been mentioned in the different blocks, this is a fresh opportunity to do so. The unit concentrates on two particularly densely packed periods when change in care policy occurred – the late 1940s and the 1980s and 1990s. By looking at your wallchart now and consulting it again at the end of your study of this unit, you will find you can make more sense of its lists of events and see how some of them connect together. If you have been marking off items as they occur, and carry on with the process now, then you should find that around three-quarters of your chart has been covered by the end of this week.

# Section 2
# The post-war settlement

## 2.1  The Beveridge vision

*It was not until after the Second World War that the British welfare state took its mature form. In a climate of relief after the war, a climate diffused with an idealism for a new, more just society, welfare legislation had bipartisan support. There was a clear sense of rebuilding a better Britain.*

(Bryson, 1992, p. 82)

These words, drawn from an Australian commentator, sum up some of the key themes of the period. There is certainly some truth in the argument that the welfare measures that were introduced in the years from 1945 to 1950 had a rather longer history. The period before the war had seen long-running debates about the lack of co-ordination of hospital services. There was concern to learn from and develop the existing experience of a health insurance scheme for medical treatment for some of the population. And there were criticisms of the legacies of the Poor Law – the indignities of means-tested payments for those in poverty and the fear among the old and impoverished of ending life in the workhouse. But the Labour government's landslide victory in 1945 (not quite as big as that in the 1997 election) was still very much about creating a new deal for 'the boys back from the front', giving them a sense that their country had been worth fighting for and would

**UNDER THE COUNTER**

support and care for them in peacetime by offering them and their families the opportunity for jobs, homes, education, health and a standard of living of which they could be proud.

The 1944 Education Act was already on the statute book when the Labour government came to power. By raising the school-leaving age to 15 and later to 16, it was going to give children chances that their parents had never had – to carry their education on (if they passed the examination) into grammar school and even to university. It would open up opportunities for jobs, homes and lifestyles that the working-class parents of these children had only dreamed of. Another nine major pieces of legislation were passed with strong support across the political parties before the decade was out. The list of legislation in the box shows that along with opportunities for access to education came a house building programme, free health services and, above all, a comprehensive programme of benefits to deal with unemployment, old age and much more besides. It was a 'brave new world' indeed.

You may like to add to the wallchart the Acts that don't appear there

---

**Main legislative measures of the post-war Labour government**

1945 Family Allowances Act

1946 National Insurance Act

1946 National Insurance (Industrial Injuries) Act

1946 National Health Service Act (implemented July 1948)

1947 Town and Country Planning Act

1947 New Towns Act

1948 National Assistance Act

1948 Children Act

1949 Housing Act

---

The architect of much of this reform in the field of social welfare was William Beveridge. His report entitled 'Social Insurance and Allied Services' was compiled as the war was at its height (Beveridge, 1942). In it Beveridge set out a plan to put an end to what he called the 'five giants' – Want (today we would call it poverty), Disease, Ignorance, Squalor and Idleness (unemployment). The centrepiece was a state-run system of *compulsory insurance*. Every worker, by contributing to a scheme of national insurance deducted through the weekly or monthly paypacket, would be helping to build up a fund that would pay out weekly benefits to those who were sick or unemployed or who suffered industrial injury. The scheme would pay pensions at the end of a working life to employees and the self-employed. The idea was to support the worker and his family. Benefits were to be set at a level that enabled a man, his wife and child to survive. There would be benefits for widows and an allowance for guardians of children without parents to care for them. A system of family allowances for the second child and subsequent children was intended to ensure that those with large families were not penalised. There was also to be a marriage grant, maternity grant and benefit, some specific training grants and a death grant. The key feature was that people were eligible to receive these benefits and grants because they had contributed. Rich and poor 'paid the stamp' and could claim as of right because of this.

For those who had not paid enough contributions or were not contributing to the national insurance scheme, there was a second tier of welfare provision, *national assistance.* The financial side of this (later to be renamed supplementary benefit and, later still, income support) was meant to be a supplement to the main scheme rather than to be central. The main scheme was universal – everyone had a right to it based on contributions. Only if supplementary help was needed did the 'means test' come into play, enquiring into your savings and your circumstances – who lived with whom, who was dependent on whom, and so on.

Alongside these financial security provisions for all, there would be universal access to education and to health services. These would be funded from taxation and would be free at the point of use. Again everyone in work would pay, but in this case, since taxation increased with increasing income, the rich would pay more. The package overall gave meaning to the proud boast that the welfare state provided care for everyone – protection 'from cradle to grave'. For it all to happen, however, there had to be full employment. The government would give top priority to the rebuilding of a strong, peacetime economy and the redeployment of troops into civilian work. Only if the workers were in work would they be contributing to the scheme.

*Beveridge addressing the public at Caxton Hall, London, 1948*

In the box on the next page are some of the comments made at the time by ordinary people who were questioned by teams of social researchers gauging reactions to the report and to the publicity that surrounded it. They will give you a first hint of the reception that Beveridge received.

**What did people think of the Beveridge report?**

Positive comments were in a clear majority:

*'It's the goods! All the yearnings, hopes, dreams and theories of socialists for the past half-century have been crystallised into a practical economic formula. Equity for the "lowest common denominator". I was staggered by its comprehension.'*

*(Insurance clerk, male, 39, Newport)*

*'It gave me a feeling there was something to work for and fight for after all and that our efforts might be rewarded by some real social improvement, giving meaning to the phrase "winning the peace".'*

*(Royal Artillery, male, 29)*

*'I am aware of a new feeling of confidence in myself as a member of a democratic society when I see those social reforms which I have considered necessary for such a long time actually taking shape.'*

*(Accountant, male, 40, Prestwick)*

But there were negative comments too:

*'My friends seem to think it's a clever piece of eyewash to retain the capitalist system by getting the people on its side.'*

*(Student, male, 22, Enfield)*

*' "A lot of blah" is the most frequent remark from the women in the factory. " Don't believe a word of it; we've 'eard these promises before".'*

*(Stores Keeper, female, 57, Winchcombe)*

*'I think it is direct encouragement to the lower type of humanity to breed like rabbits.'*

*(Temporary civil servant, female, 38)*

(Compiled from Jacobs, 1992b)

---

Activity 2    **Beveridge in his time**

*Allow about 30 minutes*

Offprint 35 by John Jacobs gives you some background on Sir William (later Lord) Beveridge and includes a vivid account of the impact of his report. Read the article now and then jot down answers to the following questions.

(a)   Why was this report so popular?

(b)   Why was insurance so much more important than assistance?

(c)   What else was in what Jacobs called the 'grand scheme of reconstruction'?

Comment    (a)   The popularity of the report stemmed from the *hope* it held out for a new future in which poverty would be abolished and no one would remain in need. It seemed to include virtually all sectors of the population and to be simpler and more far-reaching and effective than what had gone before.

(b)   The insurance principle was designed to give workers a sense of *dignity and self-respect*; there need be no shame about claiming something for which they were eligible through contribution. Assistance was designed for those who fell through the net and were unable for one reason or another to accrue contributions. Assistance benefits were *means-tested* and bore the taint of charity. Assistance, in Beveridge's view, needed to be at a lower level than insurance, otherwise people who had paid contributions would feel resentful.

(c)    Insurance was only part of a larger scheme to promote *social progress*. In order to make a full contribution to society, it was felt that individuals needed also to be protected from disease, and given access to education and housing. Full employment was crucial to the success of the scheme, and family allowances were necessary to ensure that those with children did not fall into poverty.

Writing a report is one thing – getting it implemented as policy is another. In the full article from which Offprint 35 is drawn, Jacobs (1992a) makes clear that there were a number of departures from the blueprint when the Labour government came to steering the legislation through parliament. One was a move to greater generosity. The report had recommended that the new pensions should be phased in over a period of 20 years to allow people to build up their contributions. This was the one provision that was strongly criticised, and the decision was taken instead that pensions should start being paid straight away. All the other changes rendered the provisions less generous. Marriage grants and training grants for self-employed people and those who had never been employed were discarded. Unemployment benefit was not to be indefinite but to last only for 30 weeks. Most importantly of all, given the hope to put an end to poverty, the level of all the payments from the contributory scheme, including pension payments, fell below the minimum needed for subsistence. The result was that national assistance – and its associated intrusive and inquiring bureaucracy of means testing – over the years became more important, rather than less important as Beveridge had intended. Jacobs points out that in 1990, for example, over 60 per cent of those claiming unemployment benefits either had exhausted their entitlement to benefit or had not ever been employed for long enough to build it up in the first place. The giant of Want still stalked the land.

One obvious reason why the Beveridge scheme did not ultimately abolish poverty was that the full employment assumption – which worked well through the 1950s with a buoyant economy and indeed shortages of labour – was not sustained indefinitely. Unemployment doubled between 1979 and 1981, hit a peak of over three million in the middle of the decade, and rose again in the 1990s recession (McIlroy, 1995, pp. 72–3). But there were also other changes – again for the most part ones that Beveridge could not easily have foreseen – that put pressure on the underlying principles of the scheme. Thinking back to Unit 1 on families and Unit 6 on household composition, we can see that some of the social changes that put pressure on the post-war settlement were:

- a growing rate of divorce
- rising numbers of lone parents
- growing proportions of people over retirement age.

---

**Key points**

The Beveridge report set out key principles for the welfare state:

- It stressed the need for state action in the form of income protection.
- It emphasised the insurance principle.
- It provided for health and education through taxation.
- It commanded high levels of public support.

But

- It was based on assumptions of continuing high employment and a stable family unit – hence economic and social changes ultimately put the welfare state under pressure.

---

By now, you may well be wondering why this unit is spending so much time on something that does not at first sight seem to be about care at all. But if we look a little more closely at how Beveridge justified his scheme, what he said and what he took for granted – particularly about care and caring – some important features emerge. The next section teases out some limitations to set alongside the strengths of Beveridge's vision. These limitations have left important legacies for how we understand and respond to the needs for health and social care today.

## 2.2 Did Beveridge wear blinkers?

Activity 3

**Who isn't mentioned?**

*Allow about 10 minutes*

Jacobs singled out several groups who were not covered by the insurance scheme. They include:

- unmarried women not in work (often caring for elderly parents or other relatives)
- single parents
- divorced and separated wives
- some disabled people (those who had never been able to work or who had not worked for long enough to build up a contribution record).

Can you suggest why these particular groups were outside the scheme? (Think about what they have in common.)

Comment

What these four groups have in common is that they are not wage earners and the need to carry out care or to be cared for themselves is central to their lives. For much of the twentieth century, the unmarried daughter stayed at home to care for elderly parents and may never have actually held a paid job. A single-parent mother with childcare responsibilities will find it difficult to arrange and pay for adequate childcare so that she can go out to work, so she too is often outside the labour market for care reasons. (Changes to the tax/benefit system, together with increased possibilities for childcare, however, have recently helped single mothers who are in paid work.) People with disabilities, as Jacobs points out, may never have been able to work or may not have worked for long. They too are outside the labour market, not because they provide care but because they need to receive it to some degree. Divorced or separated women are a potential exception to this – they may or may not have childcare responsibilities but, if they do, as lone parents they too will find that caring has to take precedence over entry to the labour market.

It was inevitable that groups such as these were exceptions in the Beveridge model. He had based his plan on an able-bodied man, participating in the labour market, supported by a wife who was able to provide care for children, care for him in periods of sickness and in old age, and perhaps care for elderly parents too. If the man was not able-bodied, or if the woman with children did not have a husband, the mainstream provisions of the scheme did not apply.

Do these limitations matter? If our interest is in how care gets provided, the answer is 'yes'. The individual in Beveridge's mind, the one for whom he was designing his scheme, was the working man – the male breadwinner, providing for wife and family. The key people in his scheme were able-bodied men – occasionally ill and finally old! Those who were vulnerable to repeated periods of mental illness, or had learning difficulties, or were physically disabled, suffered from chronic illness or were otherwise unable to participate in the labour market did not come on to the public agenda very clearly at all. Publicly provided 'care' entered the Beveridge vision in the shape of illness that needed medical treatment – which the new NHS would provide. He left others to fill in exactly what the reach of the new health service would be (see Section 3).

At this point let us think back to the idea of the 'five giants'. Beveridge, remember, was not just writing about income protection; he had a vision of social reconstruction and social progress. The five giants represented the key areas of need for all of us – the areas where we should pool resources to tackle our needs collectively (see the box opposite).

**TACKLING THE FIRST GIANT**

" WANT is only one of the five giants on the road of reconstruction." — T h e Beveridge Report.

| Beveridge's five giants | | |
|---|---|---|
| Want | or | The need for an adequate income for all |
| Disease | or | The need for access to health care |
| Ignorance | or | The need for access to educational opportunity |
| Squalor | or | The need for adequate housing |
| Idleness | or | The need for gainful employment |

Fiona Williams (1989) has argued that there were two more giants on the road to social progress that Beveridge did not notice. She labelled them, in words which are familiar to us but which would have been quite foreign to Beveridge and his contemporaries, the giants of Sexism and Racism. She said:

> 'When Beveridge announced his attack on the five giants – Want, Squalor, Idleness, Ignorance and Disease – he hid the giants of Racism and Sexism, and the fights against them, behind statues to the Nation and the White Family.'
>
> (Williams, 1989, p. 162)

A look at these will give us more of a perspective on what was being assumed about the range of caring work that you have been studying in this course, how it was to be handled, and why care was not clearly coming to the fore at this most important moment of establishment of the welfare state.

## More giants? Sexism

Let us leave the emotive word 'sexism' to one side for a moment and look at what Beveridge actually said about the place of women in his scheme and the kind of reasoning he used. He gave considerable attention to the position of married women:

> The great majority of married women must be regarded as occupied on work which is vital though unpaid, without which their husbands could not do their paid work and without which the nation could not continue.
>
> (Beveridge, 1942, para. 108)

This 'vital work' comprised a number of things. It included caring for their husbands and maintaining the home. Also, as you will know from studying this course, it often involved being what is now called an informal carer, looking after elderly parents and sometimes chronically ill family members. For Beveridge, however, the main component of married women's vital work was producing and caring for children. He stated:

> The attitude of the housewife to gainful employment outside the home is not and should not be the same as that of the single woman. She has other duties ... In the next thirty years housewives as Mothers have vital work to do in ensuring the adequate continuance of the British Race and of British ideals in the world.
>
> (paras 114, 117)

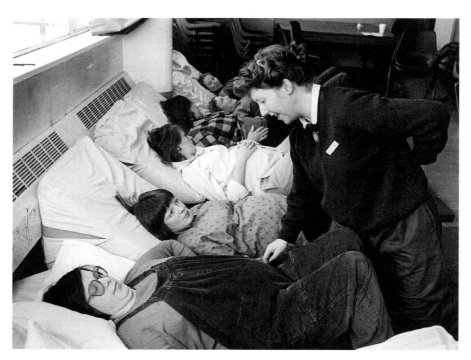

*Part of the 'vital work' of women*

It was because of his acknowledgement of the importance of childbearing and childcare, that Beveridge felt that the married woman should be entitled to economic support from her husband, both for herself and for her children. He went further and advocated maternity benefit at a level higher than unemployment benefit. This was altered after a few years, but was an indication of the importance he attributed to women's 'vital work'.

The insurance system he devised was consistent with this thinking about women. Single women would take part, like single men, in the insurance scheme. Married women would probably not work and need not do so since husband and wife together were an economic unit. If married women did work, they had the option of being exempt from contributions altogether and, if they chose to pay, they would be entitled to unemployment and sickness benefit at a lower rate, since they did not have the responsibility of family support.

| Activity 4 | **Fair to women?** |
|---|---|

*Allow about 15 minutes*

Read once more the quotations from the Beveridge report given above. Does Beveridge's approach strike you as fair or unfair to women? Jot down the reasons for your answer and see if you can also write down what arguments would be presented by someone who took the opposite view. (We will leave until a little later the question of 'the British Race' and 'British ideals' that appear in those quotations.)

Comment

If you want to argue that the insurance scheme was *fair to women*, you can point out that Beveridge recognised that women had a different place from men in society and made provision for it. He acknowledged that what women did in the home was important work – that men's economic activity could not take place without it – and he devised a form of recognition for this. His scheme thus took the reality of women's lives into account and made an allowance for the fact that they could not enter the job market in the same way as men. You could say it was fair because women were an integral part of the scheme and their different needs were recognised.

If you want to argue that Beveridge was *unfair to women*, however, you could point out that he did not treat the two sexes equally. Married women did not have the opportunity to contribute and benefit in the same way. They were seen not as people in their own right, but as wives. The scheme made them into dependants of their husbands and locked them into marriage. Family allowances apart, they were not given any financial recompense for their vital work, and their choices about doing or not doing caring work of all kinds were restricted.

At the time, many women felt that the scheme was an important advance for them, recognising them in public policy in a way that had not happened previously. Beveridge's own wife certainly took this view. In a book on the scheme published in 1954, Janet Beveridge commented that 'the whole joy of William's Scheme is its unconscious fairness to women' (Beveridge, 1954). But even at the time women's organisations and individual women came out in criticism. A pamphlet from an organisation known as the Women's Freedom League was strongly against the dependent status of women in the scheme (Abbott and Bompas, 1943), and at least one deputation to the government was organised, although with no positive result as far as the women involved were concerned (Wilson, 1977, p. 154). The next box shows that some women not only thought Beveridge unfair to women but devised a detailed alternative.

---

**An alternative to Beveridge?**

Lady Juliet Rhys-Williams, who had been an active campaigner for maternity services in the 1930s and for making family allowances available directly to mothers, proposed that each man, woman and child should have an allowance funded through taxation, payable to them if they signed a 'social contract'. Men should be available for work, unmarried women and married women without children should give some service to the community, perhaps through part-time jobs (some of which would provide much-needed help to other women with housework and childcare). The scheme was based on the principles that the state owed the same benefits to all its citizens and that no one, man or woman, 'should ever depend on any other individual for the means of existence, but only for luxuries and pleasures' (Rhys-Williams, 1943, p. 182).

If each person had an allowance and the costs of caring were shared equally:

> No woman would in future be an unpaid drudge, beholden to some relative for her living and entirely without pocket money of her own as millions of women have been in the past.

(p. 184)

She objected that the Beveridge proposals:

> do little to put right this vital matter of providing an income for wives, although the fact that wives are partners with their husbands and not mere slave-like dependants is recognised in theory by the Report.

(p. 185)

In the 1950s and the 1960s, university students of social policy learnt a great deal about the Beveridge plan and its arrangements for eligibility. I myself was one of those students in the 1960s. The emphasis in our courses was on the advances that insurance/assistance represented compared with the pre-war fragmented schemes and on the positive features of the contributory principle. Where there was controversy it was about how far the scheme redistributed from rich to poor (largely it did not – given its flat rate contributions it took more proportionately from poorer workers, redistributing their income over their lifetimes). No one at the time – staff or students – thought to ask about the impact on women and certainly no one drew our attention to the writings of women in the 1940s. It took the momentum of the feminist movement in the mid-1970s and the arrival of more women academics, before questions about women's dependency and the pros and cons of caring again emerged (see, for example, Land, 1978; Wilson, 1977; Lewis, 1983).

So was Beveridge 'sexist'? If that is a question about his motives and intentions, it is probably not a very helpful question to ask. Even the sternest feminist critics stress that he was reflecting the accepted views of his time about the role of women. He was aware of the drudgery of housework and had ideas on how to combat it; he also rejected the idea that women could be described as 'dependants' preferring to see them as 'partners' (Measor and Williamson, 1992). It may be better to think of *institutional sexism* – of assumptions built into the design of the welfare state that placed women in a distinctive and disadvantaged position compared with men and did not allow the range of work they did to be the subject of public discussion. Both the burdens and the blessings of the caring work done by women, as you saw in Unit 1, were later to become a focus, first of study, then of policy debate in the 1980s.

---

**Key points**

- The Beveridge vision relied on married women to provide care.

- It also locked women into a form of dependency that some later sought to question.

- Later, when more women began to question their traditional role, caring began to come on to the policy agenda.

---

## More giants? Racism

You may want to question whether the term 'sexism' is a useful one to help understand the Beveridge vision, but you can probably agree that there is an idea about the family and about the 'natural' responsibility of women to do caring work that kept caring off the public agenda. But this still leaves the theme of 'racism' and the idea of the 'nation'. You caught a glimpse of the importance of this a little earlier in Beveridge's confident remark about women having duties to ensure the continuance of 'the British Race' and of 'British Ideals' in the world. No public document today would contain terms such as these. The key factor that made it an important part of Beveridge's thinking, Williams argues, was the sense of national identity and pride prompted by being on the winning side in the war, and the confirmation this seemed to give that the British really were a superior nation which should be showing the way in the world and demonstrating its special sense of justice and fair play by rewarding its working classes and promoting greater solidarity.

There had been a Royal Commission on population decline, and encouraging women into motherhood was part of this national pride. So too was creating a strong sense of national boundaries and hence excluding the outsider.

This model of the men of Britain at work rather than at war, and the women of Britain at home producing children and caring for them had at least one practical flaw. There were serious shortages of labour. Part-time work for women increased dramatically in the 1950s. So did a demand for immigrant labour. A brief extract from Fiona Williams's writing will give an idea of what happened and will start to show why she says that racism and the 'statues to the nation' were built into the Beveridge proposals.

Activity 5    **Racism, 'the nation' and the welfare state**

*Allow about 20 minutes*    Read Offprint 36 by Fiona Williams and jot down your answers to the following questions.

(a)    What kinds of immigrant worker came to Britain in the 1950s and why were they encouraged?

(b)    Why were immigrant workers especially relevant in supplying jobs in the welfare state?

(c)    What examples does Williams give of the 'social costs' of immigrant labour that were often borne by the immigrants' country of origin? What do you think the term 'social costs' means?

*Comment*    (a)    Williams argues that new workers were needed because of economic growth. She says that Commonwealth citizens were encouraged in part because they were British citizens already, and the assumption was that no special welfare arrangements would be needed. ('Laissez-faire' is a French expression meaning to let things happen – in other words, do not intervene.) Williams points out that very little attention was paid to whether or not existing welfare services were suitable for newcomers – the assumption was that they would have to 'fit in' and assimilate or go back home.

(b)    Immigrant workers were crucial in staffing the NHS at all levels but particularly in low-paid manual jobs. This helped to keep the costs of services down.

(c)    Williams's two examples of the way the social costs of immigrant workers could be borne by their countries of origin were: doctors and nurses who trained before coming to Britain, and low-paid workers whose children were being cared for and educated outside Britain. The social cost of employing someone can be thought of as the full cost of enabling them to work. It is more than the wage an employer has to pay to the individual. There is the cost of educating and training the person, and there is paying them – through wages or benefits – enough to care for their dependants. There is also the matter of keeping them well, of providing for them in their old age, and other benefits that the state offers. The Beveridge scheme increased the responsibility of the state to meet these social costs for its citizens. The argument running through the offprint, however, is that the politicians wanted extra labour without taking responsibility for all the social costs (including the costs of care for dependants) and without giving full citizen rights. The politicians were also worried that popular reaction might be to see newcomers as 'scroungers' on the welfare state.

What has this to do with Beveridge? His insurance model assumed that a man would start to contribute at the beginning of his working life and emphasised that he had paid for and was entitled to the benefits he and his family later received. This required a stable population and failed to anticipate the need to recruit men and women of all ages from outside Great Britain. Although they came initially on their own, it was hardly surprising that newcomers would want to bring families and other dependants.

The insurance model also ignored established patterns whereby men and women had long been coming to Britain as a result of poverty and lack of opportunity at home. They were people who sent wages home, returned for holidays and dreamt of being able to return permanently.

*Victoria Station: labour shortages meant encouragement of immigration in the 1950s*

This was true, for example, of many Irish people. Furthermore, national insurance did not offer anything to the traveller community. Nor did it pay attention to the needs of refugees. Beveridge's wide appeal was in practice an appeal to a nation that was settled, integrated and in work. And by presenting this majority as the norm, it inevitably constructed anyone else as different and a problem. This process of defining people as 'other', different and 'a problem', was discussed in Unit 11. Mason comments:

> *Difference, particularly ethnic difference, has typically been seen as a problem in Britain. This is in part because of the tendency to assume that there was some primordial norm of Britishness from which newcomers, such as migrants, initially diverged but towards which they could ultimately be expected to change.*
>
> *(Mason, 1995, p. 2)*

Notions of inferiority of the black population have long historical roots – for example, in slavery, in colonialism and in nineteenth-century science. Beveridge did not draw on all this in a direct way – but his references to the 'nation' and 'race', together with the details of how the insurance scheme worked, served to reinforce ideas of the inferiority of the newcomers and to heighten resentments between the black and white population more generally. Starting in the 1950s, Immigration

Survey shows fewer black and Asian staff under 25

## NHS's ethnic nurse numbers decline

**David Brindle, Social Services Correspondent**

THE number of black and Asian nurses in the NHS is falling sharply despite measures to boost their recruitment, official figures suggest.

Fewer than three in every 100 nursing staff under 25 are from an ethnic minority background, according to Department of Health statistics made public yesterday by a health trade union. Fewer than one in 100 is black.

Among staff aged 55–64, however, more than 11 in every 100 are from an ethnic minority and almost nine in every 100 are black.

The MSF union, which represents many community nursing staff, described the figures as "of stunning significance".

Ute Navidi, of MSF's research department, said: "Over the years, it seems the ethnic minority workforce in the NHS has been allowed to age, while new recruits have been facing barriers to their entry into nursing, midwifery and health visiting, or have been disproportionally leaving the NHS."

(*Guardian*, 21 April 1997)

## NHS trusts hiring no minorities

**David Brindle, Social Services Correspondent**

HEALTH trusts in areas with some of the biggest ethnic minority populations have admitted their workforces are all white.

Trusts in Leicester and Bradford are among 28 which have told the Department of Health they employ no black or Asian staff. Almost 170 other trusts have failed to complete monitoring returns.

The findings have raised fresh questions about the commitment of the NHS, Britain's biggest employer, to equal opportunities. One union leader yesterday called for trust chief executives' performance bonuses to be

### 'One might detect a total disregard for ensuring equal opportunities'

reviewed if they failed to file returns.

(*Guardian*, 24 April 1997)

The data underscores figures revealed earlier this year showing a drop in the number of black and Asian nurses. The new statistics come from the 1996 census of non-medical NHS staff, which asked trusts and health authorities to code their employees by ethnic origin.

Analysis by the MSF technical union shows that whereas all but 3 per cent of organisations in the North West health region supplied their returns, 77 per cent in the Anglia and Oxford region failed to do so.

The union says a charitable interpretation of such differences would be that some organisations still [...] the capacity to log deta[...] more realistic interp[...] might detect a total[...] for ensuring that [...] policy of equal o[...] is introduced, c[...] and regularly [...]

*Concern about unequal employment opportunities for ethnic minority groups in the NHS continued through the 1990s*

Acts and Nationality Acts setting rules for who could come to Britain, and on what grounds, exacerbated racial tensions. This is something you may remember from Unit 11, where Deirdre and Benjamin came to the UK under the terms of the 1948 British Nationality Act.

Elsewhere in the work from which the extract you have just read was drawn, Fiona Williams cites evidence of the racism experienced by black people in Britain in the 1950s and 1960s in access to housing and care services, for example (Williams, 1989, p. 164). The injustices faced by some of those who came to work in the NHS in the 1950s are also beginning to emerge. One source of testimony to this comes from today's nurses who tell of gaining the necessary educational qualifications for a three-year training as registered nurses but being recruited into the two-year training as enrolled nurses from which there was no opportunity of promotion. Legislation to outlaw discrimination was introduced in the mid-1970s and amended to give more powers in the public sector recently (see Unit 11). The Commission for Race Equality has taken a number of cases against health and social services employers. Unit 11 concentrated on ways in which service delivery needs to change – and to some extent has changed – to meet the needs of a diverse population. It also referred to the question of those who work in the service. In the past, people from minority ethnic groups felt that they were discriminated against for promotion and faced racist taunts and harassment when carrying out their work. Yet they were an essential part of the labour force that allowed the health service to develop. Such attitudes persist even today (Beishon *et al.*, 1995).

Should Beveridge be called racist? Once again, we can say that he was reflecting the views of his time and that institutional racism, like institutional sexism, is deep-seated. (For a definition of institutional racism, see Unit 11, p. 98). I have been discussing not a particular agency but the policies of the welfare state as a whole. The overall idea is the same, however. It draws attention to the way discrimination can unwittingly be written into arrangements and procedures. It also shows that an idea that from one perspective has enormous benefits, from another can have deep flaws.

---

**Key points**

- The Beveridge vision of the welfare state appealed to a sense of national unity and pride in 'the British Race'; in doing so, it ignored the diversity of the existing population.

- Its insurance ideal did not easily apply to immigrants from Commonwealth countries who were encouraged to come to Britain to fill labour shortages. Nor did it relate to the needs of other migrant workers or refugees or travellers.

- The care system required them as workers but it did not pay attention to their needs for care.

- To this extent, institutional racism, like institutional sexism, was built into the welfare state.

---

It has become increasingly clear that Beveridge's notion of the citizen – the white, able-bodied working man, with a wife and family he can support through his labour and with care needs that can be met through the family unit – is narrow and much less workable than he supposed. Policy has supplemented Beveridge's model in a number of ways – as you will see in the next section – but his thinking is still present in the overall concept of the welfare state today. Summarising Section 2 as a whole, we can state that Beveridge's vision, highly influential as a basis for welfare in its time, emphasised financial support rather than public provision for caring and caring work. It left those who for one reason or another could not earn a wage themselves in a vulnerable and dependent position. Its assumptions about who was caring and how, and about women, family and nation, had the effect of consolidating inequalities of gender and race rather than challenging them. These assumptions have increasingly been brought into the open and questioned.

**Study skills:   The importance of context**

You have seen questions of sexism and racism raised in connection with Beveridge's work. Yet at the time he was seen by most as a very progressive thinker. So was he or wasn't he?

In fact, it is not an appropriate question. We are all to some extent prisoners of our times and of our own personal experiences. Nobody's ideas hold up against the judgements of all people in all times. Our capacity to think arises out of our participation in the discourses of our own times. And certainly we cannot be 'heard' by others and understood unless we speak the way *they* think. So influential new concepts and arguments are always framed within the perspectives of the time. But then later writers (in this case, Williams) revisit them and, in the process, uncover and question assumptions which had previously been unnoticed.

People have always relied on the ideas of those who have gone before, but at the same time they change and develop them. That is how knowledge advances. However, we cannot draw effectively on the ideas of past thinkers unless we are able to understand them in the context of their times. As a student you are not simply learning 'the truth'. You are gaining access to ideas, along with a sufficient understanding of their context to be able to make sense of them.

# Section 3

# Principles into practice: the development of health and social care

I have spent a lot of time explaining that the Beveridge era was about financial protection through a compulsory insurance scheme. But what did the welfare state legislation of the 1940s mean as far as actual services were concerned? The box at the beginning of Section 2.1 listed nine legislative measures taken after the Labour government came to power. Alongside the extension of free *education* (introduced earlier, under the 1944 Education Act) were the *social security* measures I have discussed, provisions for more public sector *housing*, for *health* and for the protection of *children*. Health and education services were open to all and were quickly taken up by the overwhelming majority of families. Increases in the stock of public housing provided an alternative to poor-quality, privately rented accommodation – although owner occupation through mortgages grew in popularity. Everyone in paid work contributed to the social security provisions, although some provided additional insurances for themselves privately. Many fewer would be likely to use the provisions of the 1948 Children Act, however, since it was designed for children who could not live with their families of birth.

Health care was much more visible than any other kind of care in all this. Social care, as an overall concept, was not at this point nearly so clearly thought through. In this section, I will first explore the concept of health care that was the legacy of this post-war era, looking at what it left out as well as what it included. Then I will turn to those people who needed forms of care that were not seen as health, and ask what happened to them. You saw in the last section that the Beveridge vision was blinkered as far as vulnerable groups were concerned. Now we will explore some of the practical consequences – and the legacies that are still close to the surface in today's debates about health and community care.

## 3.1 National Health Service or National Disease Service?

Alongside the new national insurance scheme, it was the NHS that became the jewel in the crown of the welfare state. Some kind of comprehensive health care system had been under discussion for a long time before 1946. However, the government had to find a way of achieving it that carried the support of powerful elements of the medical profession and ensured their co-operation. The result of complex and protracted negotiations was a service with three 'arms'.

The **hospital and associated medical specialist services** arm was the one that consumed the lion's share of the resource. The majority of the nation's hospitals were grouped together in local areas and overseen by Hospital Management Committees which reported to Regional Hospital Boards and thence to the Minister of Health. The high-status teaching hospitals in London and the big cities jealously guarded their autonomy.

They managed to keep their own Boards of Governors and a direct line to the Minister. Hospital doctors were to be NHS employees (although their contracts allowed them certain private practice sessions too).

**Family Practitioner Services** formed the second arm. GPs were the main element here, although dentists and ophthalmic opticians came under this heading also. GPs were determined not to be employees of any local authority. They remained as 'independent contractors', working on their own or in groups, loosely co-ordinated by a number of Executive Councils.

**Local authorities**, as the third arm, retained their health committees and medical officers of health who had local public health responsibilities and controlled school medical and nursing services, district nursing, health visiting and maternity and child welfare clinics. They were also charged with responsibilities for certain preventive and aftercare services for what was known at the time as 'mental illness and mental defectiveness'.

The overall structure was often called a 'tripartite structure' because of these three relatively independent components. Figure 1 sets it out in diagrammatic form.

 This organisation structure lasted for the first 25 years of the NHS in England and Wales, although the position in Scotland and in Northern Ireland differed somewhat and still does (see Care Systems and Structures).

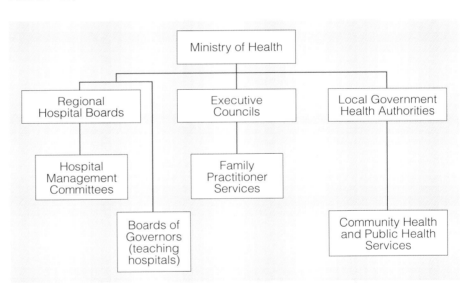

*Figure 1*
*Structure of the NHS in England and Wales, 1948–74 (Baggott, 1994, p. 83)*

Activity 6    **The structure of the NHS**

*Allow about 10 minutes*    Take a look now at Figure 1, showing the original structure of the NHS in England and Wales. Can you suggest any problems that a structure divided like this might have posed for the delivery of health care to those who needed it?

Comment    You might have spotted that co-ordination between these three arms would be tricky. GPs needed to contact staff managed by local authorities and staff managed by the NHS. Staff on hospital wards needed to be sure that there was a district nursing service available, or a bed in a residential home, but there was not much they could do to press for more resources or for services to be organised differently. These kinds of issues have not gone away and pleas for more integration of services continue to be heard today. If you have worked in the NHS or have special knowledge of it, you might also have begun to suggest some of the further points below.

A single phrase to sum up what happened would be 'hospital-centred health care'. Doctors in the acute specialities got a planned and state-supported basis from which to work – they could demand, and often achieve, the resources they wanted for new equipment and drugs. They could point to research as a priority and often had support for their wishes to implement the latest advances. Their gains on these fronts were aided by medical representation at local, regional and national level in key policy areas. There was public support for the visible results that could be achieved and faith in the potential of medical technology. Medical research, basic medical education and nurse education all took place in the acute hospitals. This meant hierarchies of prestige. Long-stay hospitals became a backwater. The doctors who went into general practice, as one eminent representative of the profession put it in a famous phrase, were the ones who fell off the ladder! Such ways of thinking did little to create good working relationships between consultants and GPs, although the latter soon began to develop their work in new ways (see the box opposite).

Hospital-centredness had its effects too on those parts of health care that remained with the local authorities. The job of medical officer of health was not as glamorous as that of clinician. Local authorities, answerable to councillors (inevitably concerned about the burden of local rates), were not necessarily going to start developing preventive health measures such as screening clinics and health education for the well population on a scale that could match what the NHS was doing for sick people in the hospitals. Social policy experts were fond of saying that the initials NHS were wrong; it was not a 'national health service' but an 'NDS' – a 'national disease service'.

The 'appointed day' in 1948 when the NHS and National Insurance systems began operation

**General practice in the NHS**

GPs play a pivotal role in health care in the UK as personal doctors. GPs refer patients to hospitals for the advice of specialists and for hospital services. Health care systems in many other countries provide for direct access to specialists and there is no general practitioner role. The presence of GPs in the UK is a result of a long historical process which was cemented by the way the NHS was structured in the 1940s.

The early years of the NHS were difficult ones for GPs. Many worked single-handedly from their own homes, trying to adapt to longer patient lists and keep up with rapid change in medical technology. Their pay was better than before the NHS but was poor compared with hospital consultants, and there were questions about the standards of care GPs could provide and about the quality of their facilities and premises. A Royal College of General Practitioners was set up in 1952; postgraduate training programmes started in 1968 and were made mandatory in 1977. New contractual arrangements in 1966 improved terms and conditions and were hailed as the 'Family Doctor Charter'.

By the 1980s, GPs working individually had often been replaced by groups of doctors and allied health professionals operating from modern premises where preventive and screening clinics and facilities for investigations were on offer. A key initiative of the Conservative government of the early 1990s was GP fundholding – whereby groups of GPs held their own budgets and purchased hospital services on behalf of their patients from hospitals who competed to win the contracts for services with them. The incoming Labour government in 1997 put the further development of this on hold while it considered criticisms about a two-tier system, in which the patients of fundholders were perhaps getting a better service than those of non-fundholders.

In a White Paper late in 1997, it was announced that the complex funding and purchasing arrangements which had developed were to be replaced. There would now be primary care groups or trusts involving all the GPs in an area, together with community nurses.

The December 1997 White Paper is on the wallchart. It is called *The New NHS: Modern, Dependable* (Department of Health, 1997). You will find more on Labour's changes to health and social care that you can see on the wallchart in Section 4.2.

**Key points**

- The NHS was shaped by powerful medical interests in the acute hospitals.
- It introduced a tripartite structure in England and Wales which was difficult to co-ordinate. In effect, it meant the dominance of hospital-centred health care.
- There have been efforts to integrate services and to focus more on prevention and on primary care.

## 3.2 Social care – poor relation of health?

What, then, happened to the many groups you have come across in this course who receive help with daily living in their own homes, or who are in residential care of some kind, or who receive various kinds of assessment that we might call 'social care'? There is agreement that this area has had a lower profile and a complex and fragmented history compared with the NHS (Gladstone, 1995, p. 161). Some elements of social care were inherited by the NHS. They included care in the long-stay mental hospitals and mental handicap hospitals as they were then called – like Lennox Castle which you saw on the Block 4 video. The NHS also took on some local cottage hospitals and certain institutions for care of older people. None of these facilities was its top priority. The acute hospitals – where health care meant *cure* rather than what seemed to be just ongoing *care* – got the lion's share of the attention and the resource. Later, as Unit 16 showed, there was press outrage about the quality of care in some of the long-stay hospitals. Means and Smith (1994, pp. 17–18) refer to a history of neglect and remind us that even at the time, not just these hospitals but services as a whole for those who were mentally ill, physically disabled, frail and old were called the 'Cinderella services'. So what happened?

Apart from the NHS, two pieces of legislation from the measures listed in the box at the beginning of Section 2.1 were particularly important for the development of social rather than health care. The 1948 Children Act meant the setting up of new local authority *children's departments*, staffed by childcare officers and under the oversight of the Home Office. The aim, in the words of the Act, was to provide 'a comprehensive service for the care of children who have not had the benefit of a normal home life'. The 1948 National Assistance Act, as you have seen, mainly provided monetary support for those who fell outside the eligibility criteria for Beveridge's insurance scheme. It also established new *welfare departments* in the local authorities along with duties and permissions to provide services for a range of groups. One section of the Act laid a duty on local authorities to provide residential accommodation for elderly people 'who are by reasons of age, infirmity or any other circumstances in need of care and attention which are not otherwise available to them'. Another section of the Act gave a duty 'to promote the welfare of persons who are blind, deaf or dumb and others, who are substantially and permanently handicapped by illness, injury or congenital deformity'. There were also at this point responsibilities in relation to finding accommodation for people who were homeless.

On the face of it, this was promising. In practice, however, it was less so. As far as older people and residential care were concerned, much of the accommodation was inherited from the Poor Law. With the same buildings and the same staff, the claim that the 1948 legislation was an Act to abolish the Poor Law sounded rather hollow. You read in Unit 8 about Peter Townsend's stringent criticisms of the quality of care for older people in these institutions in his book *The Last Refuge*. Inadequate as some of the provisions were, people also had to prove that they were without the means to support themselves. This accommodation was thus seen as a last resort and proved to be a rather poor safety-net. There were no actual powers at this point to allow local authorities directly to provide services to support older people at home. When services did come, under the Health Services and Public Health Act in 1968, local authorities were enabled but not compelled to offer services.

'Promoting the welfare' of particular client groups – the other key feature of the legislation as far as social care was concerned – was a vague term and it was interpreted differently in different places. A mental welfare officer, appointed in 1946, gives a vivid picture of the limitations of services at the time:

> *As far as the mentally ill were concerned one dealt with them by admission to hospital. There was no other way. As for subnormals, there were four of us to cover the whole county. We each had 350 to 400 cases so that they were very fortunate if they got two visits a year. We used to aim at one and a quarter, but that didn't ever come off. We didn't have the time.*

> *Of course in the early days the presence of a mentally handicapped child was frequently hidden and you didn't know the child existed. There were quite a number of people who were kept in a back room, and it was not uncommon for, if anything happened to an elderly father and mother, all of a sudden this pale face came out of the woodwork. There was nothing for them, you see. Unless they got really desperate and the family at home couldn't cope any more then they came to us of necessity to get into hospital. There wasn't any point coming forward, because we had nothing to offer.*

> (Interview with Cecil French by Jan Walmsley, October 1991)

Local authorities also often supported voluntary organisations in providing services and care rather than setting standards of what was to be done, and employing and monitoring their own staff. Behind the legislation was a belief

> *that domiciliary services were an 'extra frill' and could be left to voluntary organisations ... A complex patchwork of visiting services, day centres, meals services and chiropody did emerge but much of this provision was unevenly spread geographically.*

> (Means and Smith, 1994, p. 25)

Reading the descriptions these authors gave of a patchy meals-on-wheels service, memories flooded back to me of studying social policy, along with would-be social workers, in a North of England town in the mid-1960s. We volunteered to do a meals-on-wheels run for the Women's Royal Voluntary Service one day a week, and some people got a hot meal on that one day a week alone. There was no thinking about the standards that might be written into a contract for this kind of service today. No one had specifically taught us about values of choice and respect such as we have discussed in this course, and no one

monitored what we did. I have to admit, too, that in the case of that one hot meal per week, my newly acquired driving skills more than once landed the gravy in the custard!

 An important change in this field of work came at the start of the 1970s. The Seebohm report on social work (Seebohm, 1968) was implemented for England and Wales via the Local Authority Social Services Act 1970. A Chronically Sick and Disabled Persons Act was passed in the same year. (Similar developments occurred a little earlier for Scotland and later for Northern Ireland.)

There were to be social services departments in local authorities, generic rather than specialised social workers, and a 'single door' to all kinds of social services. Childcare departments, welfare departments and the mental health departments, which by then were also in place, were rolled into one. Teams would provide the full array of what were now to be called 'personal social services' for a designated area.

One of our course testers recalled the excitement of being a young social worker in 1971 taking up a post in one of these new social services departments. 'On the Monday morning we all changed offices', she explained. 'The old labels of children's department and welfare department had come down. I was now in Area Office 1.' While some of the staff felt daunted about their broadened responsibilities, there were some new resources. Social services departments had researchers to help establish needs. Community work initiatives would give staff a familiarity with local people and the local environment that they had not had before. The home help service could now be run from the area offices. The budget was set to increase by 10 per cent per year. But the course tester also recalled that all this was short-lived. Budget increases were cut within two years. Later, community work and community workers started to be withdrawn. Even before the new social services departments opened their doors, some commentators were saying that the design was wrong. An opportunity to put in place what could have been a 'fifth social service', tackling for individuals the poverty, the poor housing, and the lack of job opportunities that made people vulnerable and in need of personal social services, had been lost (Townsend *et al.*, 1970).

---

Activity 7   **The work of social services departments**

*Allow about 15 minutes*   Take a look at Figure 2 overleaf, which sets out the main areas of activity of social services departments as they were functioning between 1971 and 1993.

(a)   See if you are able to group these services in some way.

(b)   Identify any ways in which care services like these differ from the public provision for health and education. (Think of who they are for and how people might regard them.)

---

Comment   (a)   One way to group services is by *client group* – services for children, for elderly people, for those with physical disabilities, and so on. Another way is by *setting* – services which are domiciliary (that is, offered in the home and designed to keep people in the home), and ones which are residential or institutional. Yet another way is by *objectives* – thinking about what services are trying to achieve. Some, for example, are preventive – bolstering family life, trying to stop young people re-offending. We will return to this below. But, however you look at it, social services departments had a diverse collection of responsibilities.

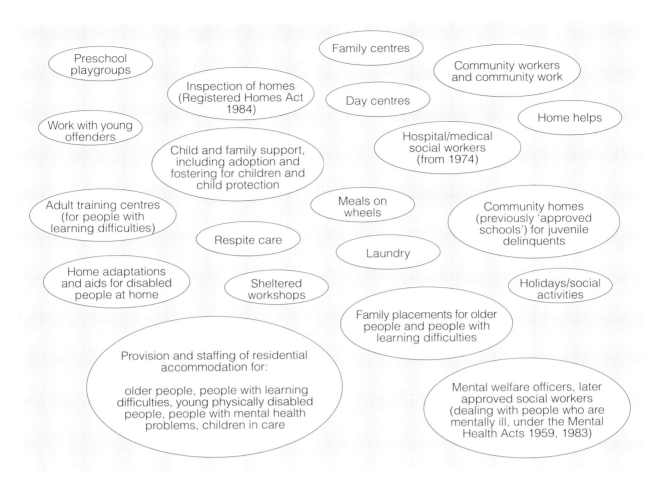

*Figure 2*
*Activities of social services departments, 1971–93 (England and Wales). Social services departments were generic, incorporating services for children, physically disabled people, older people, people with mental health problems, people with learning difficulties, and so on*

(b)   The first word that came to my mind in making a comparison with health or education was 'stigma'. Schools and hospitals were paid for from taxes and insurance and people felt they had a right to use them. Yet there were reservations about using a number of the care services in Figure 2. Some are an admission that a family cannot cope, or result from a judgement that individuals have failed in some way. Some are actually imposed on people who have not sought them: for example, when children are taken into care. I also noted another difference in this area of social care – a wide array of voluntary groups have always been involved in aspects of provision and there is perhaps a hint of 'charity' associated with them.

The nature of 'personal social services' and the differences between health and social care are discussed by Gladstone (1995, pp. 161–6). He suggests that 'stigma by association' with the Poor Law and with accepting help from charities remained a factor at the time that social services departments were established. Social workers themselves often emphasise the difference between the provision of social services (many of the areas shown in Figure 2) and the practice of social work. Furthermore, because some people have services foisted upon them (think of the child protection aspect of social work or the approved social worker in cases of mental distress), there is always a care/control dilemma, a 'difficult and delicate balance' that social workers often face.

**The Seven Ages**

*Punch depicts the Seebohm Report as offering a 'welfare umbrella' for people of all ages*

While objectives remained diverse, the new social services departments faced other challenges too. They had to bring together even more types of service and types of worker than had originally been envisaged when the Seebohm committee was set up. Organisationally, this was a nightmare. Some social workers doubted whether a generic role was feasible and many were worried about the potential loss of specialist skills in working with children.

It was children's work that had given the impetus for the formation of the Seebohm committee in the first place. And work with children soon started to dominate the agenda. Parker explains:

> *If, as professional, civil rights and financial considerations all indicated, children should be prevented from being separated from their families and ... restored as soon as possible, the issue of child protection was bound to become more prominent. The death of Maria Colwell, who was killed by her stepfather after having returned home from care, sounded an unmistakable warning (DHSS, 1974). The public inquiry that followed was the first of its kind for 30 years; but now it was followed by a veritable plethora of similar inquiries investigating child tragedies.*

> *(Parker, 1995, p. 178)*

Child protection work became a key specialism in the social services departments, with other responsibilities taking lower priority. Scandals over the treatment of children increasingly hit the headlines and the social services departments and the social work profession remained in the firing line of public criticism into the 1990s (Aldridge, 1994) and beyond. This was especially so when not only the physical abuse and neglect of children but child sexual abuse started to be of major public concern. Faced with this, the generic approach seemed misguided; social work moved back towards specialism and created specialist teams – working with children, in mental health, with older people, people with disabilities, and so on.

From very early in the 1970s, with local authorities under ever-more financial pressure, social services departments had found the bullets coming from other directions too. Were they really managing? Were they planning their services properly, were they just ever-expanding professional bureaucracies?

Government White Papers in 1971, 1975 and 1978 (see wallchart) addressed the problems of poor-quality services for the mentally handicapped, the mentally ill and older people.

There were two health service re-organisations – in 1974 (after several White Papers) and again in 1982. Throughout all this, there were repeated calls for greater efficiency and for more joint working between health and social services. The scene was set for the profound restructurings of both social care and health care which I shall discuss in Section 4.

---

**Key points**

- Social care was born in a fragmented way, divided between the NHS and local authorities in an era when NHS acute hospitals were high profile.

- Social care work encompasses a wide range of activities. It has never been a universal service like health and different aspects of it have never been very clearly spelt out.

- Policy neglect has been punctuated by scandals about the quality of services and about abuse.

- Childcare services have taken priority over care services for other groups.

# Section 4
# Back to the drawing board

By the time that a Conservative government came to power with Margaret Thatcher as Prime Minister in 1979, a great deal had changed. The confident years of economic growth that had followed the Second World War had been replaced by a very different scene. Unemployment was running into double figures, the manufacturing sector was shrinking, and Britain was falling behind other countries in measures of productivity and growth. Alongside a difficult economic situation was a set of social changes that put more demands on the public purse. I have already referred back to the points in Blocks 1 and 2 where you considered households, and families and trends, including an ageing population, more separation and divorce, and more single parents. While costs rose, headlines proclaimed it was 'Breadline Britain' for the increasing numbers claiming income support. Also, Beveridge had assumed that the NHS would clear a backlog of illness and settle down to a lower level of provision. In practice, the reverse had happened. As the range of treatments expanded, demands for health care seemed forever to be rising. In short, the public purse was emptying faster than it was being filled and public sector welfare spending was a significant part of this. Fears about escalating costs were in the air and there was a demand for greater efficiency in public services. The Labour government of the mid-1970s had started on a road to reorganising services and setting cash limits, but it was under the three administrations of Mrs Thatcher in the 1980s that a substantially new form began to take shape.

A radical rethinking, described as the 'New Right' or 'Thatcherism', emerged. It was not just health and welfare that came under scrutiny but all areas of public expenditure. In the next section I consider what New Right thinking involved, especially as it affected health and social care. This will set the scene for examining New Labour approaches from 1997 onwards.

## 4.1  Understanding the New Right

Activity 8    **New Right thinking**

Allow about 10 minutes    If someone mentions 'New Right' thinking or 'Thatcherism', what ideas come into your mind? See if you can jot down three or four items, especially as they relate to health and social care issues.

Comment    Here are some of the replies that course testers gave when we asked them this question:

- cutting public expenditure
- losing my job because we were undercut by an outside contractor in competitive tendering
- running everything like a supermarket
- making the public sector more efficient
- bashing the teachers, doctors and local government
- belief in the importance of competition and markets
- giving people consumer choice in public services.

There is quite a range in these answers. Some people have picked key words – like competition and markets and consumers, others have wrapped description and evaluation together, showing by their answer that they have a strongly held position – for or against.

What we need to do, however, is to try to identify the key beliefs and the way they hang together. One way to do this is to ask, 'How did the New Right diagnose the problem and what action did it prescribe to solve it?'

The New Right *diagnosis* was that public expenditure had been allowed to grow unchecked. As a society, the argument went, we needed to be altogether more sceptical of the idea that the state should provide. Old virtues of thrift and self-help needed to be rediscovered and the 'nanny state' should be eradicated. What threatened to be a growing burden of publicly funded provision for old age was a particularly important factor – people should be cared for in families, or they should be encouraged to make their own financial provisions for the risks of illness and disability and for care in later life.

In broad terms, there was a series of related themes here, among them the notions that:

* central planning had generated large, costly and *inflexible bureaucracies*
* *people* had become *dependent* and lost the will to help themselves
* *professions* had had too much freedom to shape services, they had become *unresponsive* to their clients and their arguments for growth had been accepted uncritically
* *public sector workers* had held the country to ransom for increases in wages; indeed, all *trades unions were 'undemocratic'* and their power should be restricted
* left-leaning *local authorities* had been too *profligate* with their spending.

The New Right *prescription* involved bringing in thinking from the commercial world – the discipline of the private sector marketplace – to the functioning of state services. First, a new kind of management was needed, people with an entrepreneurial spirit, people who would use the management tools of business and ask whether things were being done in a cost-effective way. Such people, it was thought, would monitor output, ask about the 'bottom line' (of the balance sheet) and not be afraid to take on the professionals as well as the trade unions. Second, the public sector itself needed to be shaken out of its complacency as a monopoly supplier. It was competition, the New Right argued, which kept quality up and costs down in the private sector. Market competition therefore had to be introduced in some way into the public sector too.

Behind both the prescription for more active management and the prescription for markets was a notion, as one observer put it, that government had grown 'too big, too expensive and too inhibiting of enterprise' (Pollitt, 1990, p. 48). Welfare state provisions were seen as an integral part of the problem of a state that had become bloated, that was slow-moving, complacent and wasteful.

This thinking led to a major programme of change in many different spheres. Nationalised industries and public utilities were transferred into private hands, civil service functions became the province of newly independent agencies, services that had been provided by the central state or by local authorities were put to the test of the marketplace through competitive tendering. People started to find that the menu in the hospital canteen bore the logo of the firm that had won the contract rather than the name of the hospital, that the laundry service for residential homes was the responsibility of a newly formed private agency, the school cleaner was employed by a firm that was only interested in the school as so many metres of floor space to clean at a competitive price.

'Rolling back the state' is a phrase that sums up the strategy of the New Right and the many changes of the decade. In practice, it was not just the Conservative governments in Britain in the 1980s who adopted this major reforming stance as far as welfare was concerned. Economic crises and rising demands for care services forced governments of many other countries in similar directions (Gladstone, 1995, p. 23).

What did this mean for health and social care? Before 1990 health authorities had both planned and delivered care. Funding for services came from the centre, health authorities were monitored to ensure that they kept within budgetary and service guidelines, and staff were employed on NHS conditions. Social service departments too, as you saw in the last section, had provided a wide range of direct services to client groups. Now health authorities and social services departments were to become purchasers – that is, they were to assess needs within their areas and arrange to supply them by issuing contracts to others. Those who wished to provide care services would bid to do so, with the purchasers periodically inviting competitive bids and commissioning services. A look at the wallchart for 1989-90 will show you that the key ideas of this period were introduced first through the publication of White Papers, before being confirmed in legislation.

The changes make a great deal of sense seen in the light of the New Right 'diagnosis' set out earlier in this section. We can take each of the five points (on page 99) in turn.

- *Bureaucracies* were to be transformed by creating purchasers with a contract mentality who would search for efficient providers rather than administer a service they themselves provided.

- The *'dependency culture'* was challenged by stressing people's need and wish for independence and the government's role in supporting that.

- The *professions* would have less influence in deciding priorities: in community care, the new care managers would not necessarily be social workers or make social work assessments; in health care, markets would put doctors' comparative performance under scrutiny (although there was a bigger role for one set of doctors through GP fundholding).

- With the possibility of purchasers contracting with alternative providers, unionised *public sector workers* would be in a less strong position.

- *Local authorities* would take a lead in social care but they would be planning and purchasing services rather than always providing them.

*Health care goes to market*

At the time, there were both pessimists and optimists about the New Right reforms. The *pessimists* argued that the main problem of both health and social care services was that they were under-resourced. They saw money that could have been used for care being poured into setting up the new systems. They saw caring work being pushed back on to the shoulders of unpaid carers. They predicted that employers of low-paid staff in the private and voluntary sectors would inevitably try to undercut each other to gain contracts and so would reduce workers' pay even further. The *optimists* regarded things differently. Change, they argued, was badly overdue. It was good to shake up the complacency of the institutions of the welfare state, which had neglected to consider outcomes and costs and to pay attention to efficiency and effectiveness. The new arrangements freed up thinking and promised real innovation and choice for users.

 So who was right? Much was written in this period about the impossibility of real market relationships and the inappropriateness of thinking about people in need of care as 'consumers' who would and could exercise choice (see Unit 10 and Chapter 29 in the Reader). Sometimes the internal market did mean more creative and appropriate solutions to care needs were found. But too often, service users could feel as if they were involved in a game of 'pass the parcel' – as care managers, and private and voluntary providers struggled to make limited resources go round (Langan and Clarke, 1994, pp. 83-4). You will find one worker's view on this in the Reader (Chapter 32). Take a look too at the introduction to Section 5 of the Reader which comments on the new regime of the New Right and also offers a caution about how far Chapter 32 is representative.

## 4.2 Labour's response – new-style health and social care?

Labour came to power in 1997 after 18 years of government by the Conservatives. So was it 'back to Beveridge' or was it 'business as before', continuing with the New Right approach? Put in another way, did it mean faith once again in *the state* as provider of services, or did it mean keeping the essence of *the market* approach? The answer of Prime Minister Tony Blair was that it would be neither of the old models. New Labour, as it came to be called, was going to pursue a 'third way' for welfare and for public services.

What exactly did this mean? I shall take an example from health and an example from social care to start to tease out an answer. Action on health came first. Six months into office, in December 1997, the Labour government unveiled its White Paper on 'the new NHS'. It insisted that there was to be a new start.

> *There will be no return to the old centralised command and control systems of the 1970s. That approach stifled innovation and put the needs of institutions ahead of the needs of patients.*

(Department of Health, 1997, Para 2.1)

But if the strong state was not the solution, the market was not the solution either. Here is a paragraph that could not be plainer:

> *The internal market was a misconceived attempt to tackle the pressures facing the NHS. It has been an obstacle to the necessary modernisation of the health service. It created more problems than it solved. That is why the government is abolishing it.*

(Department of Health, 1997, para 2.9)

Labour did not want to be guided by what it saw as old dogmas of the right or of the left. Instead, it wanted to build on what had been shown to work and to discard what had not. 'What counts is what works' was a key phrase repeatedly used by ministers and liberally sprinkled through the policy documents. GP fundholding was one thing that Labour felt had not worked. In its place there was a vision of new primary care trusts planning for a whole area. Added to this were some entirely new ideas, such as NHS Direct – a telephone advice service led by nurses. The value of walk-in centres and one-stop shops perhaps in the supermarket or the railway station and again with new roles for nurses also started to come onto the agenda. On the other hand, Labour saw some merit in the Conservatives' purchaser/provider split. Instead of a return to controlling everything from the centre, there would be local level planning. Primary care trusts would commission services for their areas as well as being providers. Health Improvement Programmes, drawn up with social services' involvement – trying to mend that historic split between health and social care – were now on the cards. All this was to happen in the context of centrally set targets. Locally there would be freedom to develop services but this must occur, the government insisted, inside a framework of better quality, efficiency and accountability. The overall health of the community and the reduction of health inequalities was not forgotten. A consultation document came in the following year, and a White Paper *Saving Lives* followed.

A social services makeover emerged next. *Modernising Social Services* was the title of a further White Paper in November 1998. One underlying problem, Labour felt, was a lack of clear standards.

*There is no definition of what users can expect, nor any yardstick for judging how effective or successful social services are. Individuals do not know what services are available, in what circumstances they might get them, or whether they will have to pay.*

*(Department of Health, 1998a, para 1.4)*

The White Paper set out a vision of services that would be more consistent and better co-ordinated across the country, and would respond better to diverse needs and offer more effective protection to children and vulnerable adults. 'Quality Protects' was a newly funded programme of service improvement for children and a Social Services Modernisation Fund was put in place to enable other initiatives to take place. Stronger partnerships across health and social care, and a new body to train and register all workers in the care field were among the many other proposals.

One term that was used repeatedly was 'modernisation'. The new NHS needed to be modern. So did social services (see Unit 8). The regulation of the professions had to be modernised (see Unit 26). *Modern Local Government* was the title of yet another White Paper (DETR, 1998). So can we dig any deeper into this?

Activity 9  **Making public services modern**

*Allow about 10 minutes*  What does 'making services modern' mean to you?

(a)  First, think about your pet hates about the health and social care services that you, or perhaps members of your family, have experienced. You may have been frustrated or perhaps angry about how you were treated. You may have found yourself comparing your experience with public services with the way you are treated in private sector service industries.

(b)  Can you pinpoint any changes – drawing from your own experience – that have meant that things have become more modern in some way?

Comment  (a)  Too much waiting, the dingy and sometimes dirty conditions, the lack of good facilities, the sheer inconvenience of trying to get appointments and get routed through the system – are these perhaps some of the main things you listed? A large-scale consultation in the run-up to the publication of a wide-ranging NHS Plan (Department of Health, 2000) found that all of these were important to people. Also on their lists were: more staff, with better pay and better conditions of work, higher quality services in areas such as cancer and heart disease, more help and information on healthy living and a guarantee of high quality services wherever people lived.

(b)  One change that I thought of immediately that seemed to make things more modern was NHS Direct the nurse-led telephone help-line. This new source of easy to access advice for members of the public, as we have noted, was announced in the Labour government's White Paper on the NHS.

So what does modernisation mean? High quality services responding to a more demanding, better informed and busier public seems to be at the heart of it. Government determination to get waiting lists down, to put the NHS on the information superhighway, to get many more staff and to bring in new ideas for accessible and timely services all link to this.

A great deal has now happened under the banner of 'modernisation'. The box lists some of the many new bodies that have been created. But instead of you trying to remember what all these new agencies and approaches are and to keep up with change in every area, the point is to understand the directions of change. I would single out five of these.

1.  **More standard setting from the centre** – New national 'institutes for excellence' are reviewing just what evidence there is for different services and, in the health field making decisions about rationing costly medical procedures. National Service Frameworks in areas such as cancer care, care of older people, mental health and so on are setting out a model of good practice that all services need to meet. Targeting funding to particular programmes is another means of focusing service providers on specific outcomes that the government wants to see.

2.  **Stronger monitoring and reviewing** – There has been a massive and continuing shake-up in arrangements for regulating the people and inspecting the places where health and social care takes place. There have been new bodies and amalgamations of new and old as the government has tried to create a streamlined and effective overall framework. We can think of 'hit squads' with a focus on grading performance and 'help squads' with a stress on demonstrating how best practice could be embedded more generally. (You met this topic in Block 6.)

3.  **Reorganisation with a primary care focus** - The creation of primary care trusts, the formation of strategic health authorities in England, and the different moves in other parts of the UK have the same underlying purpose. This is to get away from hospital-centred health care and to emphasise instead the promotion of healthy living and the prevention and early treatment of disease.

4.  **Working across boundaries** – New procedures to help social services and the NHS to work together to provide continuity of care have been introduced. Both sets of services in some places have come together so that staff are employed by a unified care trust. Working across traditional occupational and professional boundaries is also being stressed in projects to change and develop the workforce. Keeping and encouraging private and voluntary sector providers to give patients a choice is also very much on the Labour agenda – watched with scepticism by some trade unions, as a full page advertisement taken out recently shows.

5.  **Involving citizens and service users** – This is now a major theme in just about all government documents. There will be more on it in Section 5.

*Illustration GMB advertisement*

---

**Labour: changing the landscape of health and social care**

Here are just a few of the new national bodies set up under two terms of Labour after 1997:

- Social Care Institute for Excellence

- General Social Care Council

- Council for the Regulation of Health Professions

- National Institute for Clinical Excellence

- Commission for Health Improvement

- National Institute for Clinical Excellence

- Modernisation Agency

Add to these the creation, for example, of Primary Care Trusts, Strategic Health Authorities, the importance of National Service Frameworks. Add another raft of new ideas in 2002, including foundation hospitals, diagnostic and treatment centres, the reorganisation of even some of the very newest bodies to create the Commission for Healthcare Audit and Inspection and the Commission for Social Care Inspection (see Unit 8, p. 126). Factor in the idea of an NHS Bank - and you might well think that we are close to needing a wallchart as big as the one for the 20th century for the years since 1997 alone!

If you want to know more about these changes, the legislation which has been occurring, and the growing differences between the different parts of the UK, refer to Care Systems and Structures.

---

Not surprisingly, there have been complaints that Labour has been much too interventionist. The press talked of 'control freaks' and of efforts at 'micro-management' from the centre. One influential pair of commentators on health policy refer to what they call 'relentless, almost hyperactive intervention' and they add:

> *A formidable torrent of pledges, policy documents, laws, regulations, advice and guidance has issued from the Department of Health, without let-up since 1997, to knock the system into shape ...*

> *Appleby and Coote, 2002, p. 5*

The torrent continued after the first couple of years as room was made for new legislation to put changes in place. For health care, the NHS Plan announced in 2000 brought many old and new proposals together in a document of nearly 150 pages (Department of Health, 2000). And in 2002, coinciding with announcements of substantial further funding in the Budget, more adjustments and changes were put in place (Department of Health, 2002). Some of the new bodies hardly started before their powers and responsibilities were changed! (see box). This has contributed to a sense of overload, particularly, Appleby and Coote note, on the new primary care trusts, which they see as pushed to the limit by this torrent. Much the same could be said of those working in social care.

So what does it all add up to? Taking a long view – across the whole of this unit - it is clear that health and social care services have faced two decades and more of relentless pressures for change. There have been repeated reorganisations over the years. I suggest that there have been three distinct periods:

- the RISE of the state – in the post-war era with the Beveridge plan

- the REJECTION of state action – in the 1980s under the internal market ideas of the New Right

- the RE-EMERGENCE of the state – under New Labour from 1997.

*The budget of April 2002 increased rates of national insurance to pour more money into the NHS – raising the political stakes and the government's determination that modernisation would be visible to voters before the next election*

The form of this re-emergence was still being worked out in Labour's second term of office. The New Right had objected to the 'nanny knows best' welfare provider state of the 1940s and tried to roll it back and make people stand on their own feet. The New Left tried to keep the idea that the state should not provide it all, and that people should make choices. But in doing so, it became a regulatory state, introducing standards, targets and monitoring as never before. Just what it meant by the 'third way' in providing welfare and public services has proved difficult to pin down, but this new emphasis on regulation is part of it.

**Too cynical?**

Many writers have tried to find a way of encapsulating the approach of New Labour by naming its key ideas. Martin Powell, an influential health policy analyst, however, casts doubt on such an exercise. He observes that Labour responded to the situation it had inherited by simply keeping what seemed to work. In place of big ideas, he suggests 'PAP' – pragmatism and populism. Pragmatism is captured in the favourite phrase 'what matters is what works'. And populism means not persuading and leading the electorate, but wooing it and bending to it – running the focus groups and adjusting action and spinning the news accordingly. In short, Powell concludes 'the big idea is that there is no big idea' (Powell, 2000, p. 53).

**Key points**

- The Conservative governments of the 1980s and early 1990s transformed arrangements for the delivery of health and social care by introducing the idea of markets, purchasers and providers.

- New Labour in 1997 brought both continuity and change with its determination to 'modernise' and its emphasis on quality and standards, monitoring and performance review.

- Health and social care services are very much in the spotlight and are under immense pressure to adapt and change.

Whether fundamental priority shifts are now under way remains in question.

One important feature of New Labour's programme for the modernisation of public services that we have not examined, however, is its stress on the involvement of people both as users of services and as citizens who should have a say in how services are run and what they provide. Is there a strong pressure for reshaping services and priorities now coming from this direction? This is the final topic for this unit.

# Section 5
# User voices – absent, present or on the way?

How can people be sure to get the care services that they really need? How can you know that what will be offered is adapted to your own particular values, needs and circumstances at the time? One point that this unit brings out is that there have been at least two very different answers to these questions.

In the 1940s, when Beveridge was the great architect of welfare state reform, a big part of the answer was 'give the job to the professionals'. There was faith in the extent to which governments could co-ordinate a nationwide scheme of provision, ensuring that relevant specialist skills were available in all parts of the country. The NHS was the epitome of this. The highlight of it was the hospital services arm and a bureaucratic machinery at local, regional and national level was devised to ensure that everyone had access. Doctors were represented at all levels of policy making and the bureaucrats listened to what the doctors had to say and deferred to them. If, as a user of services, you had a strong view on how those services should be shaped and what should be spent on them, your main recourse was the ballot box at the next general election. You cast a vote for a party and for its programme for health and social care as set out in its manifesto. You also had some say at local level by voting for those councillors who would sit on the health and welfare committees of the local authorities.

Under Conservative governments, the answer shifted dramatically towards 'let the consumer decide'. The intention was to put a lot more information on comparative performance of services into the public domain, to break monopoly provision and give the consumer altogether more choice. In the main, however, as you have seen at different points in the course, this consumerism often works at one remove. The person buying the services is not the patient but the GP or care manager making decisions on behalf of the individual, or the social services department or health authority devising contracts and purchasing services for a local community. This is one way in which the pure 'consumer' model is limited. Another is that people with limited resources, feeling vulnerable and under stress, are not in the best position to become assertive and critical consumers, as Baldock and Ungerson showed in their study of people who had suffered strokes in Kent (Chapter 29 in the Reader). But the mood was definitely changing. You have already seen at different points in the course, the way that expectations about services have been rising and criticisms and calls for different approaches have emerged. A consumer movement grew in strength in the 1990s as organised groups of patients and service users began to make demands nationally. Government stressed that patients and the public needed to have a say in how health services were organised and provided locally and started to demand to see the results of consultations with Community Health Councils and local voluntary organisations (NHSME, 1992). Labour's call for modernisation after its return to power in 1997, played down the term 'consumer'. But it certainly demanded that services be more responsive to user needs. Whether this was more of the same or something different as far as user involvement was concerned, is a question I will tackle later.

So do users and potential users now have the power to be heard in the planning of care and in the management of care services as well as in individual decisions about their own care? The answer is probably 'yes', but a cautious 'yes', since the question of how to involve users and carers effectively is still under debate and the shift of power that this entails will not necessarily come about smoothly.

Activity 10    **Promoting user involvement in service planning 1**

*Allow about 10 minutes*    Imagine that your local NHS trust has taken a decision to gather consumer views about the future direction of cancer services in its large general hospital. The trust board has agreed that a public meeting would be a useful step. An advertisement is put in the local newspaper inviting people to attend on a Thursday evening in July. Leaflets have been prepared and sent to all GP surgeries and to the main and branch libraries. The local radio station has agreed to announce the meeting. The plan is that the senior oncology consultant will open the meeting by describing the work of his unit. Someone from finance will then explain the budgetary situation and the hard choices the trust has to make. Then 'the floor will be open', as they say, for comments and suggestions. The next morning both the trust staff and the people who attended are disillusioned and angry. What do you suppose went wrong?

Comment    You might have found yourself wondering just who would be likely to respond to an invitation like this. The hall might be very empty. The timing would be good for some but would exclude others. Who would come and why would they come? People with an axe to grind about how a relative or friend was treated might be there. Some would be carers, perhaps some would be cancer patients, and others might have come out of general

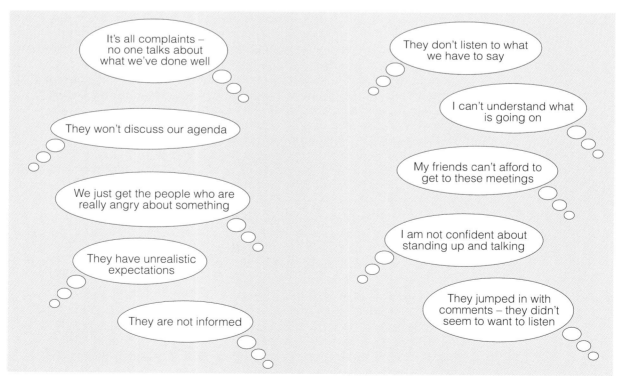

*Figure 3*
*User and provider views of services can be in conflict with each other (adapted from Goss and Miller, 1995, p. 34)*

interest. It would be hard to predict who the audience would be. People would not know each other and speakers would not know what kind of an audience it was. The 'think bubbles' on the opposite page are a summary of some of the negative reactions that might occur from those on the platform and those on the floor.

A 'doom scenario' will not always occur, but there is a quite a volume of research that suggests that reactions like this are not uncommon. The 'quotes' opposite are fictional but are based on a study that monitored several user involvement projects and was designed to encourage the development of user- and carer-centred community care (Goss and Miller, 1995). This study made practical proposals for what could be done to establish two-way communication – what resources and facilities had to be offered to users to enable them to participate, and what changes organisations had to make in order that providers could really listen and make use of what they heard. The ineffectiveness of the big public meeting, and the weakness too of simply sending out consultation documents and inviting written replies are now being recognised. There are many examples across the country of schemes of involvement, which work in a different way. The box based on user panels in Fife gives just one example.

---

**Fife user panels project**

Users and potential users of community services for frail elderly people were identified jointly by health and social service providers and by Age Concern Scotland (ACS). People had to be over 75, live on their own, and have a health problem or a disability (excluding dementia). Seven user panels were set up during the first three years of the project (1992–5) and the project was then extended. Panels of around six to eight people met monthly supported by ACS staff. New members were recruited as numbers fell as a result of illness and death.

The group began by discussing growing older – good and less good aspects of daily life, and their definitions of quality. They used games to stimulate thinking about priorities, developed an imaginary case study to focus on how a care package could be developed, and after a time had the confidence to invite statutory agencies to meet them and discuss services. They developed a 14-point 'Good Hospital Discharge' checklist. They also responded to requests from health authority staff to help with the design of a questionnaire and of information leaflets for older people.

The researchers found that, after taking part, about half the participants were characterised as more positive on measures designed to explore their sense of control – something they felt was encouraging, given the decline in health and mobility that many would be experiencing. Panel members said that they valued the opportunities the meetings gave for learning from one another and giving them a sense that they could contribute to service change. One 90-year-old woman said, 'It has given me courage'.

*(Barnes and Walker, 1996)*

Activity 11    **Promoting user involvement in service planning 2**

*Allow about 10 minutes*    (a)    List ways in which the Fife project differs from the public meeting
strategy you have just considered.

(b)    Then see if you can jot down its underlying assumptions about what
makes participation work.

Comment    There are several contrasts you might have noticed here.

- The project was concerned with a specific user group, not the public
as a whole.

- Time was set aside for building the group and enabling people to get
to know one another.

- Facilitators were on hand with ideas about how to get discussion
going.

- The group was an ongoing one.

- It began with a broad and open agenda, allowing people to compare
notes on what their priorities were, and only later coming to specifics.

Overall it is clear that the organisers were working to ensure that attending
the group was a rewarding experience in itself. They were not assuming
participation would happen – instead they were being active in helping
people to express their views.

Barnes and Walker (1996, p. 380) argue that a theme of *empowerment*
underlies this kind of development. They define empowerment in a
broad way as 'the process of enabling excluded and minority groups to
exert greater autonomy in decision-making'. They discuss what it means
to empower the 'quiet voices' of frail elderly people (you might think of
the example of Millmead on the Block 4 video) and whether
empowerment for users necessarily means a loss of power for
providers. Those who provide services can easily feel threatened by
developments like this, and Barnes and Walker argue that it is important
that the provider organisation is ready to change its working practices
and particularly to support its front-line workers, who can all too easily
be squeezed and 'scapegoated' when user expectations are raised by
new forms of participation in service planning. The decision by the
service user group, the College of Health, to provide training for people
who were going to act as lay voices together with the professionals and
managers is one response to this. You might remember that it was
mentioned at the end of Unit 26.

Public meetings and user panels are by no means the only ways of
making service user voices heard. Agencies have long had suggestion
boxes and carried out surveys to check satisfaction with services,
although we can now perhaps see that these are not very empowering
ways of involving users. Independent research can bring the worldview
of user groups vividly to notice. (Chapter 19 in the Reader by Jenny
Morris under the title of 'Creating a space for absent voices' was
deliberately intended to do this; so too was Chapter 13 by Ruth Pinder.)
This is not the same as people speaking for themselves, but you have
read throughout the course about advocacy projects and self-help
groups who take the initiative and are now sometimes working closely
with providers on questions of policy. Some authorities are also
experimenting with new ideas. Block 6 discussed all this in some detail
and Unit 24 referred to 'citizen's juries' of local people, giving them
evidence to weigh up and helping them to come to a decision about a
new policy. As the material on the Fife user panels showed, people can

become highly engaged with the issues and also make dramatic changes in their views when part of a process like this.

One way to think of all these mechanisms is to ask about the stages in the planning and care delivery process that people might be involved in. In Unit 22, Activity 4, you explored this in the context of a discussion of self-advocacy. Another way of thinking about it is offered by the concept of a ladder of user and carer involvement. First introduced in the USA in the context of partnership in town planning (Arnstein, 1969), it has become widely known and used (see Figure 4). On the bottom rung there is no involvement at all – decisions are taken inside the organisation and nothing is done to secure feedback on how services are working or on changes that people might like to see. On the next rung is the provision of information – annual reports, leaflets, perhaps meetings and discussions, all designed to make people aware of services and how they might use them. The third rung, a step further, involves people by testing out plans the organisation has already devised and getting answers to questions the organisation has decided are important, whereas on the fourth rung, users and carers can add items to the agenda and suggest ways of tackling problems; in both cases, though, it is the organisation that decides what to take forward. The fifth rung means direct involvement in all aspects of policy making on a joint basis, whereas on the sixth rung:

> the agency hands over the setting of the agenda, decision-making and the steering of the implementation process to users and carers. This either involves the formation of user- and carer-controlled organisations or users and carers managing staff ... who then provide advice and do the leg-work.

(Goss and Miller, 1995, p. 65)

The ladder diagram underlines how user involvement is about the power to take decisions and where that power lies. Where would you place the Fife user panels project? You explored its strengths compared with the public meeting in Activity 11, but it is not on the top rung, nor is it probably on the next one down. It is not very clear whether power to shape services was actually transferred to the panels, and it looks as if it was not. The same questions could be asked of other initiatives. Take the growth, for example, of patient participation groups in GP practices, or the use some local authorities and health authorities have made of specially constituted citizens' juries, set up to debate a hard choice about what to fund and what not to fund in a local area.

Since Labour came to power in 1997, yet more steps have been taken to bring user voices into the design and running of public services. Local authorities now have a duty to consult local communities and government policy aims to be much more 'in touch with the people' (DETR, 1998). There are regular user and carer surveys as part of the 'Best Value' inspection regime for social services in local areas. England's Chief Nursing Officer was given the additional title of Director for Patient and Public Involvement. Late in 2001, she explained how the components of this involvement were intended to hang together and she stressed the central importance of the new overarching Commission which was to take a lead (see box).

A year earlier, the wide-ranging NHS Plan for England had set the scene for developments over the next decade. It was not just the new measures on user involvement that were interesting – it was how the Plan had been produced. The build-up to the final document included:

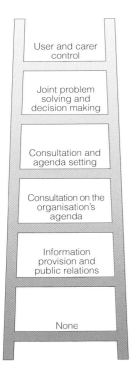

*Figure 4*
*The ladder of user and carer involvement (Goss and Miller, p. 65)*

User and carer control

Joint problem solving and decision making

Consultation and agenda setting

Consultation on the organisation's agenda

Information provision and public relations

None

- A large-scale public consultation exercise to identify and confirm priorities
- Involvement of patient representatives and staff in a series of preliminary Modernisation Action Teams to generate and discuss ideas
- The gathering together of a diverse group of those who had been involved to sign the report and show commitment to the directions it was taking. More than a third of the 25 signatories represented patient and carer groups (including among others the Carers National Association, The Patients Forum, The Long Term Medical Conditions Alliance, Alzheimer's Society and Diabetes UK).

New developments were not confined to England. In some ways it was easier for a smaller population group for communication and dialogue between the centre and localities to occur (for details see Care Systems and Structures).

Alongside all of this, the many new national bodies that Labour created in the health and social care field (see box on page 106) had lay representatives in membership. You have already seen in Unit 26 how new moves were made to bring greater lay involvement into the bodies regulating the professions. All in all, things were starting to look very different from the 'give the job to the professionals' approach of the Beveridge era. With opportunities for participation and dialogue now in so many places, it also seemed things were going beyond 'let the consumer decide', the choice in a marketplace approach of the New Right.

---

**A new phase in patient and public involvement?**

Following what the government called a 'listening exercise', it was announced that the new patient and public involvement strategy for the NHS in England would include:

*Patient forums in every NHS trust and PCT*

- to seek out patient and carer views, to monitor local services and inspect services. They would report to the trust board and elect a member to join the board.

*A Patient Advisory and Liaison Service (PALS)*

- to help individual patients and carers where they needed it.

*Overview and Scrutiny Committees*

- a new power for local authorities to examine whether NHS services meet local need.

*An Independent Complaints Advocacy Service*

- a reorganised system for assisting people to make complaints about NHS services.

*The Commission for Patient and Public Involvement*

- an independent national body, setting standards, providing training and acting as a source of advice through a system of local networks.

*(Presentation to Harrogate Management Centre Conference 'Patient and Public Involvement in the NHS', 11 December 2001, Barbican, London.)*

Is this a complete transformation of how policy decisions are made nationally and locally? CHCs – set up back in 1974 and due for abolition under the new arrangements – had a lot of concerns. They were worried in particular about the independence of the bodies and about the potential loss of valuable experience. Researchers began to sound warnings about changes on paper versus changes in practice. The challenges

- of involving more than the 'usual suspects' and of bringing in hard to reach groups

- of helping appointed lay people work out how to be more representative

- of enabling patients, public and carers to have a real impact and not to be sucked in to an organisational way of looking at things

are all still there. 'Every Voice Counts' was the title of a study bringing experiences together. It concluded that while there was good practice to report, the matter of making every voice count was still far from being resolved (Anderson, Florin, Gillam and Mountford, 2002).

What conclusions can we draw about policy and politics in health and social care? It is certainly no longer true to say that user voices are absent from policy discussions in health and social care, but perhaps it is still too soon to say that all such voices – especially the 'quiet voices' – are fully present.

---

**Key points**

- There have been important moves towards greater user involvement in policy making in the health and social care services.

- There are examples of users not only being involved in decisions about their own care but also of planning services and monitoring and evaluating them.

- For this to work well users need to be empowered and service providers may need training and support to reconceptualise their roles.

- The question of whether we are at the beginning of a new era of more diverse contributions to policy making in health and social care is still open.

# Conclusion

The first core question for this unit asked:

**What are the underlying ideas which prompt state provision of health and social care?**

Beveridge's answer, which won much support in its time, involved a bargain. The citizen (an employed man) would contribute through insurance and in return the state would provide education, specialist health services and income protection. This responsible citizen would thus be able to provide financially for his family, and that family (in the shape of the married woman), in turn, would provide much of what today we call social care. You saw the weaknesses in this as an idea and also the ways in which it was overtaken by events.

In the 1980s a different answer emerged. The all-protecting, paternalistic state was out of favour. Beveridge's bargain, it was believed, had created dependence and added to escalating costs. The state needed to pull back. The idea of responsible citizenship now was that people needed to provide more for themselves, and family responsibilities needed to be reaffirmed. Citizens also started to be seen less as people with rights to a state service and more as consumers in a marketplace, making their own decisions and entitled to choice. Labour has now tried to find a third way between the monolithic services of a paternalist state and the wish to bring in market competition. A strong state role has re-emerged in terms of setting national standards and close monitoring. At the same time it is trying to keep some choice for service users and freedom for providers to develop local services in ways that they see fit.

The second core question was:

**Who influences the direction care services are taking?**

Answers to this question may be changing. Research reports showed ordinary people (for the most part) as deferential and accepting of the Beveridge report. Today there would be questions about who was consulted and more active lobbying by organised care groups. Labour governments since 1997 have extended this theme, bringing a number of service user groups into the policy process centrally and locally. That brings us to the third and fourth questions, namely:

**Do services respond to user needs and offer real choices?**

and

**Has sufficient priority been given to groups who are likely to be neglected?**

An important lesson from this unit is that there are many players in the policy arena and different groups lead at different times. The unit suggested that the NHS was doctor-led until recently, and that under the Conservatives, there were efforts to make it more manager-led. More space has opened up in recent years for user voices to be heard, but we also now have strongly interventionist governments trying, as some people put it, to 'micro-manage' services from the centre. The unit also suggested that social care was overshadowed by the health and disease agenda and that this is a struggle we still face today.

It would be possible for you to tackle the question of how far services respond to need without reference to the historical factors discussed in this unit. The aim, however, was to show you that legacies of past thinking about policy remain and that new thinking builds on the past and does not always escape from it into something entirely new. By discussing the assumptions which have underpinned policy, we can start a process of bringing them into the open and getting to a broader perspective on what has been achieved and on what remains to be done. I hope you agree.

---

**Study skills:   Tactics in the exam**

You have already thought about your revision strategy and about how to build yourself up towards a 'peak performance'. Finally, you need to think out very clearly how you will organise yourself in the exam itself. Again it's worth doing this in advance because you may be too busy and too keyed up later. So read Section 6 of Chapter 7 of *The Good Study Guide* now. (You will have to make a few adjustments as you read, since it talks about a paper which requires answers to four questions and you only have to do three.)

Here are two things to do when you have read Section 6.

1   **Answer-planning technique**. Look back carefully at Figure 7.2 to make sure you have the principles fixed in your mind. Also look back at Section 4.2 of Chapter 7. Then work out how you are going to set about practising your technique. You will soon run out of questions on the specimen papers, but after the first year of K100 you should be able to get hold of past papers. Another possibility is to team up with a fellow student and set each other questions; or your tutor may be able to help. But do try to get plenty of practice in developing a rapid response to questions. It's a different mode of thinking from the more measured, contemplative approach to a TMA question. You need only enough ideas to keep yourself writing for 45 to 50 minutes – but you must be able to jot them down quickly.

2   **A time plan for the exam**. Draw yourself a plan of the kind shown in Figure 7.3. It will have to be different, because you are writing only three answers. (The one I sketched starts the same, but writing the first answer ends at 11:05, and then I allowed 10 minutes each for planning the other two answers.)

Having seen exactly how much time you have for thinking and writing in the exam, you can now be even more focused in your revision. Now you know what you are trying to achieve. Your revision notes for the units of your chosen blocks only need to assemble the main ideas and enough information and case material to be able to write 50-minute answers.

# References

Abbott, E. and Bompas, K. (1943) *The Woman Citizen and Social Security: A Criticism of the Proposals of the Beveridge Report as they Affect Women*, Women's Freedom League, London.

Aldridge, M. (1994) *Making Social Work News*, Routledge, London.

Anderson, W., Florin, D., Gillam, S. and Mountford, L. (2002) *Every Voice Counts: primary care organisations and public involvement*, King's Fund, London.

Appleby, J. and Coote, A. (2002) *Five Year Health Check: A Review of Government Health Policy 1997-2002*, King's Fund, London.

Arnstein, S. (1969) 'A Ladder of Citizen Partnership', *Journal of the American Planning Association*, Vol. 35, No. 4, pp. 216-44.

Baggott, R. (1994) *Health and Health Care in Britain*, Macmillan, London.

Barnes, M. and Walker, A. (1996) 'Consumerism versus empowerment: a principled approach to the involvement of older service users', *Policy and Politics*, Vol. 24, No. 4, pp. 375–93.

Beishon, S., Virdee, S. and Hagell, A. (1995) *Nursing in a Multi-Ethnic NHS*, Policy Studies Institute, London.

Beveridge, J. (1954) *Beveridge and his Plan*, Hodder and Stoughton, London.

Beveridge, W. (1942) *Social Insurance and Allied Services (Beveridge Report)* (Cmd 6404), HMSO, London.

Bryson, L. (1992) *Welfare and the State – Who Benefits?*, Macmillan, Basingstoke.

Department of the Environment, Transport and the Regions (1998) *In touch with the people: modern local government*, (Cm. 4014), The Stationery Office Ltd, London.

Department of Health (1997) *The New NHS: Modern, Dependable* (Cm. 3807), The Stationery Office Ltd, London.

Department of Health (1998a) *Modernising Social Services: promoting independence, improving protection, raising standards* (Cm. 4169), The Stationery Office Ltd, London.

Department of Health (1998b) *Our Healthier Nation* (Cm. 3852), The Stationery Office Ltd, London.

Department of Health (2000) *The NHS Plan. A plan for investment. A plan for reform* (Cm. 4818-1), The Stationery Office Ltd, London.

Department of Health (2002) *Delivering the NHS Plan. Next steps on investment. Next steps on reform*, (Cm 5503), The Stationery Office Ltd, London.

Department of Health and Social Services (1974) *Report of the Committee of Inquiry into the Care and Supervision provided in relation to Maria Colwell*, HMSO, London.

Gladstone, D. (ed.) (1995) *British Social Welfare: Past, Present and Future*, UCL Press, London.

Goss, S. and Miller, C. (1995) *From Margin to Mainstream: Developing User- and Carer-Centred Community Care*, Joseph Rowntree Foundation, York.

Hills, J. and Lelkes, O. (1999) 'Social Security, Selective Universalism and Patchwork Redistribution', in R. Jowell, J. Curtice, A. Park, K. Thomson, with L. Jarvis, C. Bromley and N. Stratford (eds) *British Social Attitudes: The Sixteenth Report*, Ashgate, Aldershot.

Jacobs, J. (1992a) 'An introduction to the Beveridge Report' in Jacobs, J. (ed.) (1992) *Beveridge 1942–1992: Papers to Mark the 50th Anniversary of the Beveridge Report*, Whiting and Birch Books, London.

Jacobs, J. (1992b) 'December 1942: Beveridge observed. Mass observation and the Beveridge Report' in Jacobs, J. (ed.) (1992) *Beveridge 1942–1992: Papers to Mark the 50th Anniversary of the Beveridge Report*, Whiting and Birch Books, London.

Land, H. (1978) 'Who cares for the family?', *Journal of Social Policy*, Vol. 7, No. 3, pp. 257–84.

Langan, M. and Clarke, J. (1994) 'Managing in the mixed economy of care' in Clarke, J. *et al.* (eds) *Managing Social Policy*, Sage, London.

Lewis, J. (1983) 'Dealing with dependency: state practices and social realities, 1870–1945' in Lewis, J. (ed.) *Women's Welfare, Women's Rights*, Croom Helm, London.

Mason, D. (1995) *Race and Ethnicity in Modern Britain*, Allen and Unwin, London.

McIlroy, J. (1995) *Trade Unions in Britain*, Manchester University Press, Manchester.

Means, R. and Smith, R. (1994) *Community Care: Policy and Practice*, Macmillan, Basingstoke.

Measor, L. and Williamson, V. (1992) '"Vital work to do". The implications of the report for women' in Jacobs, J. (ed.) (1992) *Beveridge 1942–1992: Papers to Mark the 50th Anniversary of the Beveridge Report*, Whiting and Birch Books, London.

National Health Service Management Executive (1992) *Local Voices: the views of local people in purchasing for health*, Department of Health, London.

Parker, R. (1995) 'Child care and the personal social services' in Gladstone, D. (ed.) *British Social Welfare*, UCL Press, London.

Pollitt, C. (1990) *Managerialism and the Public Services: the Anglo American Experience*, Blackwell, Oxford.

Powell, M. (2000) 'New Labour and the Third Way in the British Welfare State: A New and Distinctive Approach?', *Critical Social Policy*, Vol 7, No.1, pp. 39-60.

Rhys-Williams, J.E. (1943) *Something to Look Forward To: A Suggestion for a New Social Contract*, Macdonald and Co., London.

Seebohm, F. (1968) *Report of the Committee on Local Authority and Allied Personal Social Services* (Cmnd 3703), HMSO, London.

Taylor-Gooby, P. (1991) 'Attachment to the Welfare State' in Jowell, R., Brook, L. and Taylor, B. with Prior, G. (eds) *British Social Attitudes: the 8th Report*, Gower, Aldershot.

Townsend, P. *et al.*, (1970) *The Fifth Social Service*, Fabian Society, London.

Travis, A. (2002) 'Popularity of Budget halts Tory Revival', *Guardian*, 23 April 2002.

Williams, F. (1989) *Social Policy: A Critical Introduction*, Polity, Oxford.

Wilson, E. (1977) *Women and the Welfare State*, Tavistock, London.

# Acknowledgements

Grateful acknowledgement is made to the following sources for permission to reproduce material in this unit:

## Text

*P. 85 (left):* Brindle, D. 1997, 'NHS's ethnic nurse numbers decline', *Guardian*, 21 April 1997, © Guardian Newspapers 1997; *p. 85 (right):* Brindle, D. 1997, 'NHS Trusts hiring no minorities', *Guardian*, 24 April 1997, © Guardian Newspapers 1997.

## Figures

*Figure 1:* Baggott, R. 1994, *Health and Health Care in Britain, p. 84:* Macmillan Press Ltd, with permission; *Figures 3 and 4:* adapted from Goss, S. and Miller, C., *From Margin to Mainstream, p. 65*, Joseph Rowntree Foundation.

## Illustrations

*P. 72:* ZEC/*Daily Mirror*/Syndication International/Centre for the Study of Cartoons and Caricature, University of Kent, Canterbury; *pp. 74 and 84:* Hulton Getty; *p. 78:* George Whitelaw/*The Daily Herald*/Centre for the Study of Cartoons and Caricature, University of Kent, Canterbury; *p. 80:* Maggie Murray/Format; *p. 90:* 'The 'appointed day' in 1948', Report to the Nation No. 20, Crown copyright is reproduced with the permission of the Controller of Her Majesty's Stationery Office; p. 93: Maggie Guillon; *p. 96: Punch*; *p. 105:* © 2002 GMB. Reproduced by permission of GMB Britain's General Union; *p. 107:* John Kent cartoon, News International syndication.

# Unit 28
# Course Revision and Review

Prepared for the course team by Celia Davies and Andy Northedge

Updated by Andy Northedge

While you are working on Unit 28, you will need:

- Course Reader
- Offprints Book
- *The Good Study Guide*
- Audio Cassette 7, side 2
- Media Notes

You will also find that you need to refer to the whole set of course materials when carrying out the revision exercises here.

# Contents

# Introduction

*'The course has been great – but I'm really nervous now about the exam!'*

*'What do they expect? How can I possibly hold it all in my head? It was hard enough when I had one block to think about, let alone having seven of them at once!'*

*'With the TMAs, I could refer back to the material while I was writing. What am I going to do now?'*

If these are some of the things you are thinking as you come to this final unit, rest assured that you are not alone. This unit has been designed to help you with the process of reviewing the course as a whole, consolidating what you have learnt – and, most importantly, putting the exam in proportion! By the time you have worked your way through it you will find that you are much more familiar with the various blocks and are perhaps starting to make new links between the material in them.

The unit contains:

- an *overview of the process of revision*; this is accompanied by a set of activities – taking rather longer than you are used to – to get you into revising actively for yourself.

- *a consolidation of the work you have done on study skills*, reviewing the progress you have made and what you can now take ahead to future courses.

- finally, a *discussion of themes and issues* that have emerged through the course; this will help you to form a picture of the course as a whole and to remind yourself of some of the many things you have studied in the past seven months.

The aim at this stage is not to give you yet more information but to enable you to make more of the knowledge you already have. To do this you need to review your own learning. While no one else can do that for you, the unit is designed to help keep you on track and perhaps offer a shortcut here and there.

# Section 1
# Preparing for revision

Revision in its most simple sense means looking again at something, familiarising yourself afresh with something you have seen before. But if you look again at all 27 units, turning over hundreds of pages, you will soon feel you are drowning. As you have read in *The Good Study Guide,* revision needs to be an active process – looking again, but with a particular purpose in mind. You might ask yourself 'If I had to summarise this in five main points, what would they be?' Or you might write down all the key points for a particular unit or section of a unit and say to yourself 'If I have really grasped this, then it should be possible to jot down a brief explanation of each key point in my own words in another one or two sentences'. Or again, you might ask yourself 'Who are the most important writers on a particular theme in a block? What is the main point made by each one of them? Are they agreeing with and complementing each other, or are they in conflict?'

All of these are ways of making revision an *active process* – you are engaging with the material and setting up a dialogue with yourself in relation to it. Learning, as *The Good Study Guide* says, is not a matter of cramming facts into your head. It is:

- *Taking in new ideas (... making sense of new ideas, not simply 'hearing' and 'memorising' them).*

- *Thinking through new ideas* and fitting them alongside your existing ideas so that you build up a better general *understanding* of the subject you are studying.

- *Expressing newly formed ideas* by talking and writing about them.

*(p. 13)*

There is nothing new about this. You have worked throughout the whole course with the idea that learning is an active process, and that you need to do something in addition to just reading. The course has been peppered with activities. Sometimes they have come at the very

beginning of a discussion, asking you to consult your own experience, to see how your initial thoughts might be different from those of other people and how you can build on this for the purposes of studying a topic. Sometimes we have asked you to read something, then summarise it and comment on it. Even the most experienced student can find their mind wandering when faced with the task of just reading page after page of text. So it is with revision. Briefly glancing at the course materials, dipping in and rereading can be useful, but you will find that you need to be more purposeful and to have a strategy that makes you engage with the materials if you are really to consolidate what you have learnt and be able to remember and reproduce it.

Activity 1  **The course at a glance**

*Allow about 45 minutes*  Imagine that someone has asked you whether they should take the course. No doubt your first move will be to warn them about what hard work it is! What they want to know, however, is what kinds of things are actually in the course – what topics they would find themselves studying.

- Taking two sheets of paper, write out the seven block headings, leaving roughly equal amounts of space under each one. In your own words, describe each block in not more than three or four lines below the heading. If you find your mind is a blank on one or more blocks at this stage, don't worry, just move on to the next one.

 • Now, try the same activity again, this time allowing yourself to consult the actual blocks. You will probably find it helpful to look at the block introductions, the unit contents lists, the core questions, and perhaps the final few pages. A glance at the illustrations can be a good way of jogging your memory too.

Comment  Trying to produce a summary (even a very short one like this) without the materials in front of you is a tall order. You probably found that some blocks came to mind much more readily than others (and there may be a clue there as to where you will need to put extra revision effort). Summarising with a contents list and introduction in front of you, however, is not as easy as it seems. You still have to prioritise and you probably found it was easier where you could actually recall the material directly.

Different people will highlight different aspects of the course, so there is no 'right' way of describing each block. If you wish, look back at the Introduction and Study Guide where there is a brief description of each block. But the important thing is the way in which the exercise focuses your mind, allowing you to distance yourself from the material and to ask what it is really all about.

You have now taken the first step in active revision. You have a couple of sheets of paper that set out the course at a glance and you have done it in your own words. You may find it helpful to redo this 'course at a glance' document as you revise particular blocks in detail or as a result of other exercises in this unit. You might want to use your 'course at a glance' document in other ways. For example, you could set a revision timetable down one side of it and check off your progress in covering the materials.

Don't be afraid to spend time writing things out again. Revision notes often become messy as you add further thoughts and jottings. Time spent in producing another version is rarely wasted – it helps you to fix things in your mind. Tidy notes also encourage you to go back to them on another day. Remember, though, that people revise differently. If some of the strategies suggested in this unit sound useful to you, then use them – if they don't, then find a different way!

What is next? How are you going to get into the materials in more detail? In the first place, you will need to remind yourself of the range of materials you have got. The main course units are your key resource, but there are other things too. However, you won't have time to look at everything in detail, so go down the list below and decide which you think you will try to look at again and in what order. (Write numbers against them to remind you of the order.)

- The main course units
- The skills units (Units 5, 9, 13, 17, 21 and 25)
- Articles in the Course Reader
- Articles in the Offprints Book
- The wallchart
- Care Systems and Structures
- Your notes on activities
- Your notes on readings
- The audio cassettes
- The specimen examination paper
- The video cassettes
- Your study diary
- Your portfolio (if you have one)
- The Introduction and Study Guide
- The Media Notes
- The introductions to sections in the Reader
- The TMA guidance
- Your essays and feedback from tutors.

A reorganisation of your notes might be useful at this stage. If, for example, you have notes on activities, you might want to pull out those activities that asked you to make notes on readings so that you can give them more priority. You might decide to make a list of the audio cassette themes and the names of key participants, but to set the actual tapes to one side for now. How do your notes on readings look? Might it be worthwhile to look through them, put a star against some of them and set aside time to read them again? Which you choose will be a personal matter, but some of the headings come up several times and so form links between the topics of the different units.

## Activity 2  Reorganise!

*Allow at least 30 minutes*

Perhaps it is time to put this unit on one side for a while and concentrate instead on reorganising your study materials. A good 'tidy up' can often be a first step in reminding you of all that you have studied, and nothing interrupts your train of thought more than having to hunt for notes that seem to have gone missing altogether. Almost inevitably you will want to do some reorganising at this stage, since you need to handle all seven blocks instead of just one.

This might be a matter of half an hour or it might take much longer. You will need to clear some space so that you can gather all the course materials around you. If you didn't quite manage to take the advice in *The Good Study Guide* about having your own space, keeping your notes in order and filing material away in clearly identifiable sections, now is the time to have another go. Spread the materials out in piles so that you can see what you've got.

Now the end of K100 is in sight, perhaps you can negotiate afresh with those who have been encroaching on your study space. You can promise that it will all be packed away quite soon!

Comment

Some people go out and buy all kinds of box files and folders, sticky labels and coloured pens to help gear themselves up for revision. Others keep what seems to be an untidy pile of material – but they know how to lay their hands on something in it.

To go alongside your 'course at a glance' document, you might like to compile some of the lists already mentioned – of key readings, of who was who on the cassettes. Or, for a different approach, try Activity 3.

Activity 3

### Quick Quiz 1

*Allow about 20 minutes*

If you have pulled your notes on readings together and marked up those you think you might want to return to in the course of the revising, then attempt Quick Quiz 1 below. There is no 'right' answer but we have given one course team member's response to this in the appendix at the end of the unit.

**Quick Quiz 1: Your 'top ten' readings from K100**

You have read a wide variety of material for this course – policy documents from statutory bodies, newspaper cuttings, articles from professional and academic journals. They were all focused on a very specific point of discussion in the unit at the time, but some of them were more important than this. They drew together key strands of thinking or they challenged orthodoxy and heralded change. Some things were referred to several times in different blocks.

Which readings – from the Course Reader or the Offprints – would you single out as the key ones, and why?

So far you have been 'warming up'. But how will you set about some actual revision? On the first half of Audio Cassette 6 you heard some experienced OU students saying what they did. You might want to go back and listen again for ideas. Alternatively, let's imagine some different approaches that students might take.

> *'I'm a fan of the highlighter – I use one colour on my first read, and then go through when I'm revising with a second colour to make the key points stand out.'*

> *'I go through a process of reducing my notes, summarising and summarising; I aim to have one sheet of paper in the end for each block, crammed full of key writers, key facts, key ideas – perhaps with a quotation or two which I think really gets to the heart of the matter.' (See the diagram on page 222 of The Good Study Guide.)*

> *'I am someone who thinks in pictures – I do charts and spider diagrams – I try to put the argument in boxes with arrows going between them – it oversimplifies but that's what helps me to get the essentials into my head for the exam.'*

> *'I'm going to use the wallchart. I'll work down it finding the bits I've marked and go back to the units if I need to remind myself. Then I'll draw up a simple version for myself.'*

> *'I actually type out a set of summary notes – otherwise I find I just don't want to look at my messy handwriting!'*

> *'With K100 we've got it made – all those core questions and key points. For each unit in the blocks I'm focusing on, I'll photocopy the contents page. Then I'll go through the unit highlighting two or three words in each key point and use those to write a brief version of the key points under each sub-heading on the copied contents page. I'll also note where the main case studies and readings come. Then I'll have created an overview of the unit on a single page.'*

On the next page is an example of the third of these approaches, applied to Unit 1. I asked Andy Northedge to do this. He commented:

> *I drew it fairly quickly by working from the unit contents list. I put the unit title in the middle, and the five section headings around it. Then I put the subheadings branching off from the main headings and added in a few other details. Notice that I used my own words instead of just copying. This makes it feel like my version, not just a routine exercise. Sections 4 and 5 of the unit need a little more work. You can try adding those bits for yourself.*

Of course, how you go about revision is entirely up to you. What all these suggestions have in common, though, is that they involve more than just memorising. It is for you to reflect back on what has worked for you up to now with K100 and then think of some techniques to try.

The 'golden rule' of revision is to *create a revision plan*. This means allocating your time, prioritising your tasks and knowing how you work best. You may have started work on this already, following the study skills discussions in the earlier blocks. But if you have not done so yet, you really need to start now. You need to ask yourself:

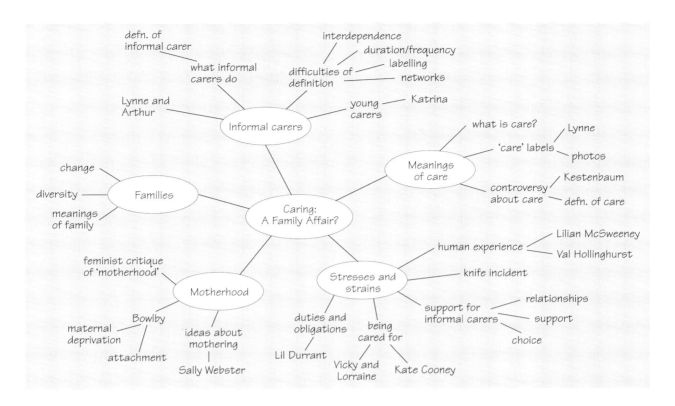

- Roughly how many study days and hours do I have between now and the exam?
- Which blocks am I going to focus on for the exam?
- Realistically, what is the maximum time I am going to spend on any one block?
- Which of the materials am I going to concentrate on for my chosen blocks?

To help you put timings on the various elements of revision it is worthwhile to carry out the next activity in full.

Activity 4    A revision taster

*Allow about 2 hours*

Give yourself a substantial period that you will spend on one particular block, I am suggesting two hours. Choose one of the first three blocks because they are a long way back. Let's say you choose Block 2. Plan to allocate 30 minutes to each of Units 6, 7 and 8, and 30 minutes to review your achievements. You might find it helps for this exercise to set an alarm or a timer to keep you on track.

You have already browsed the materials for your 'course at a glance', so you have reminded yourself what is in the various units.

- For Unit 6, try highlighting words in the key points. Then jot down a list of all the key points in your own shortened versions – and note the case studies and readings from which they arise.
- For Unit 7, take three sheets of paper and head them 'key themes', 'key information' and 'key writers'. See if you can then write down relevant points on each sheet. You might, for example, find one or two short quotations from the readings which encapsulate a message well.
- Think up a strategy of your own for Unit 8.
- Use your final half hour to review how much you were able to achieve in your 30 minute periods using these different strategies.

Work out what this tells you about how to use the rest of your
revision time.

Comment  How did you get on? I don't expect you feel absolutely on top of Block 2
after just this activity. It was about getting your revision strategy right,
rather than getting your revision done. You might decide that key points
really work for you – or that it is much more useful to do your own
summarising along the lines suggested, or in some other way altogether. I
hope, however, that you are persuaded that doing something other than
just reading is worthwhile. Whatever the outcome, you have made a start
on your revision. There is less of it to do than there was two hours ago.

However you decide to work with the blocks, you will still want to vary
your activities from time to time. Rereading key readings is one thing,
checking out your knowledge is another. Whatever you do, keep an eye
on the calendar. Keep marking up your revision plan and revising it as
you go along. It really does not matter how many versions of it you
draw up.

On the next page are some more quizzes for you to use later on in your
revision if you think they might be helpful. You might like to do them
now and again later to check your progress. Help with the answers is
given in the appendix.

**Quick Quiz 2: Who wrote what?**

Name the subject of each author's writing and the block in which it appears.

1    J. Wallcraft

2    R. Shah

3    L. Doyal

4    B. Duffy and B. McCarthy

5    F. Williams

6    J. Killick

7    Dartington Social Research Unit

8    D. Willcocks, S. Peace and L. Kelleher

**Quick Quiz 3: Who is or was ...?**

Henry Mayhew

Lady Rhys-Williams

Erving Goffman

Lady Gillian Wagner

John Bowlby

Peter Townsend

Erik Erikson

William Beveridge

**Quick Quiz 4: What is meant by ...?**

Defensive practice

Emotional labour

Vulnerable adults

Scripts

Active consumerism

Private space

Stereotypes

Identity

Informal carers

Institutional racism

Self-advocacy

Self-help groups

Sick role

Social exclusion

Disabling environments

Eugenics

New professionalism

Institutionalisation

Community action

Social Darwinism

The New Right

New managerialism

Behavioural programmes

Normalisation

---

**Key points**

- Revision is an active process.
- Organising your course materials is crucial.
- Make a revision plan (and keep updating it).
- Bold, sweeping summaries are what you need at this stage.
- Develop ways of revising that work for you.

---

To end this session and start pointing you towards the exam, the final audio cassette of the course introduces you to two students talking about how they have turned themselves into experts at taking exams.

Activity 5　**Doing the exam**

*Allow about 30 minutes*　Listen to Audio cassette 7, side 2.

Comment　I hope you found something useful in the strategies suggested by these students. Bear in mind that they are at the end of their Open University studies and are more advanced than you can reasonably expect yourself to be right now.

**Study skills:　Final points on exams**

Some reminders about planning:

1. Don't allocate all your revision time to revisiting the blocks. Allow time for activities such as sketching out practice answers.

2. You may find yourself functioning rather differently in the final couple of days (see Chapter 7, Section 5 of *The Good Study Guide*) so don't leave your basic coverage of key units till then. Aim to switch into an overviewing, consolidating and question answering mode.

3. You may need a more detailed plan for the last week to make sure you clear enough time with family, employers and anyone else.

4   Don't forget to sketch a time plan for the exam itself.

It might help to listen to the discussion on side 2 of Audio cassette 7 again, to remind yourself how those students handled the run up to exams. They also wrote down these tips for you about the exam day itself:

- If you revise thoroughly there is nothing to worry about.
- Put pens and other things you need for the exam together beforehand.
- Prepare for the journey to the exam – double check your transport.
- Relax the night before.
- Arrive in plenty of time.
- Take deep breaths before the exam.
- Don't panic when you read the questions.
- Read the paper twice and take three deep breaths before answering anything.
- Read the questions through carefully – a few times if needed.
- Underline key words.
- Before beginning answers, brainstorming is a good way of remembering most topics.
- Plan your answer – e.g. a spider chart.
- Remember all the other students are in the same boat.

Finally, it's worth skimming back over Chapter 7 of *The Good Study Guide* so that you are thinking strategically and creatively as you start this last big heave towards the exam. In fact, you will find that there is a short piece – Section 7 – that you haven't been asked to read yet. I hope it will encourage you to keep yourself in a realistic but positive frame of mind.

I asked Andy Northedge, author of *The Good Study Guide* and of the study skills boxes you have used throughout this course, what he would want to say to you about consolidating study skills. As a result, he wrote the following section.

# Section 2

# A review of your study skills progress

Having arrived at the end of the course, it is time to look back and see how your skills as a student have progressed since February. You might be tempted to wait till after the exam before taking time for this. However, once the exam is over, you will probably have a strong urge to put K100 behind you for a while. And anyway, thinking about your skills may help you with your exam preparations. So here are some things to try.

| | |
|---|---|
| *Activity 6*<br><br>*Allow as long as you think appropriate* | **Pulling together your work on study skills**<br><br>(a) Revisit the 'half way' review in Unit 13, Activity 10. Using a different colour pen, fill in the 'Now' column again. Then see what changes there are. How does your progress in the second half of the course compare with that in the first half? Have you made progress in different areas this time?<br><br>(b) Use the skills listed in the table in Activity 10 as headings to write down the left of a sheet of paper. Add 'exams' and 'confidence' to the list. Then get your study diary and reread it from the beginning, making notes under these headings. When you have finished, try to summarise what is under each heading.<br><br>(c) Look back over the comments on all your essays. (You did this before in Unit 21.) Write notes summarising your strengths and weaknesses and the progress you have made.<br><br>(d) You should now have read just about all of *The Good Study Guide*. Skim back over Chapters 1–6, dipping in where something catches your eye, but mainly just reading the key points and tips. Think how you might continue to make use of the book for your next course.<br><br>(e) Write yourself a review of your study skills under the headings<br>• main areas of progress<br>• aspects needing further work<br>• specific plans for development of skills on next course (remembering that you will probably not be getting advice then, so you will have to work out plans of your own). |

| | |
|---|---|
| *Comment* | There is a lot to do here, but how much is up to you. You are the one who knows best how much progress you needed to make when you started K100, and how much there is still to do. |

## 2.1 The main study skills

### Reading

You should feel very practised now at launching into a wide variety of reading – with a pen or highlighter in hand – and a clear eye on what you want to get from the reading and the time you can allow for it. No more sitting and wallowing hopelessly like Michael (pages 3–4 of *The Good Study Guide*).

## Studying audio-visual material

You have listened to seven audio cassettes and watched two video cassettes and a TV programme. Were they worth the time? Thinking back, do you find that material particularly vivid and easy to remember? Were you able to learn things that would have been difficult to absorb from a written text? Were you able to use what you learnt in your assignments? Are there lessons to take forward to future courses regarding the time you need to allow or techniques for getting the most out of these more free-flowing media?

## Note taking

You have been encouraged to take lots of notes, using a variety of techniques, from jotting on the text to drawing spider diagrams. How useful does it all seem now? Do you feel you have developed an effective personal style which helps you get quickly to the 'bones' of the ideas and information you encounter – or do you still need to experiment some more?

## Numbers, tables and charts

After all the exercises you have worked through and the TMA questions, do you now feel more confident about finding your way around tables, charts and graphs? Can you remember anything useful and/or interesting that you learnt from the charts and tables in the course? How helpful did you find the technique of starting from just one number and telling yourself what it means? There is still plenty more to learn, but the essential first stage is to be able to approach numbers constructively and *make* them make sense.

## Learning with other students

How much use did you make of the tutorials or day schools? Did you form a self-help group or any other working links with fellow students? How valuable was the contact you had? What aspects of study did it help you with? Your future OU courses are likely to have fewer and more scattered opportunities for student contact, so if you want the benefits of collective working you will be more reliant on your own initiative and enthusiasm. If you think it is important, make plans.

## Organisation and time management

Together these are the key to success, especially for part-time and distance students. To come this far you must have worked out some pretty effective practices. But perhaps, looking back over the course, you can see some important lessons for another year – times when you let the schedule slip, or when you let one thing take too much time so that you had to miss out another. Time and the unexpected events of life always cause problems, but experience and an ability to plan strategically certainly help.

## Keeping up morale

Perhaps this isn't the moment to review your morale, with the exam just around the corner. However, you must have steered yourself through many ups and downs during the year. I hope it has become clear just how important it is to keep your studies in perspective and above all to enjoy them as much as you can. In the long term, guilt and fear are seldom effective motivators for distance students. You learn best when you build on your strengths and when you treat your studies as an opportunity to find out what *you* want to know.

### Essay writing

You must surely feel you have made significant progress with your writing (even if you were quite good to begin with). It would be very strange if months of practising and receiving feedback didn't make an impact, especially with all the reading and reflecting using *The Good Study Guide*. But with writing there is always more to aim for: advances in style and fluency, techniques of gathering and organising material, new kinds of writing (reports, projects, papers). And perhaps, if you are not doing it already, it is worth thinking about word processing for next year. If so, can you plan in a couple of months of regular practice with a computer program to teach you to touch-type? In any case you are bound to be able to build on the skills you have developed this year. Perhaps greater writing skill is the most valuable thing you have gained from K100?

### Exams

Maybe you should leave your review of this for now. However, I hope you already feel you know a lot more about exams than you did a couple of months back.

### Overall

It is a core aim of K100 that you should develop a wide range of study skills to a point where you can be successful on degree courses at Levels 2 and 3. With all the advice you have received, and the encouragement to experiment and reflect, you must surely have achieved that objective. Give yourself congratulations and a suitable treat!

# Section 3
# Thinking about the themes of the course

K100 has been a very broad-based course of study. It has considered a highly diverse set of people involved in care and caring, some paid and some unpaid. It has covered both health and social care. It has taken you into many different settings – family homes, residential care settings, hospitals, day centres and care facilities of many other kinds. It has given examples of good and bad practice in caring. It has, as the wallchart shows, spanned a century of care and indeed at times has gone further back in drawing your attention to the poor law and the institutions that were created as part of that. In doing this, it has given you an insight into the contributions of several of the social sciences. You have read material by sociologists and psychologists, historians and social policy specialists, and been encouraged to read (and to read between the lines of) policy documents and guidelines to tease out implications for the care that people might receive.

So how can you now bring all this together? To help you begin to form an idea of the course as a whole I am going to talk you through three overarching themes which I see running through the course. There are other ways of drawing out themes from a course as wide ranging as K100, and we will mention a couple later, but these are the main messages which come across to me.

- *Theme 1: the complexity of the concept of care* – the many facets to caring and being cared for. An important argument here, and one that runs through much of the course, is that care has been neglected and devalued through assumptions that it is something ordinary and simple. This occurs particularly through the idea that care is 'women's work', that it just 'comes naturally' to women and hence does not need to have attention paid to it.

- *Theme 2: the dilemmas of care relationships* – how understanding of these has progressed and how skills can be developed. Under this heading we can place the many challenges that have come from people on the receiving end of care – often what they are looking for is more recognition of their individual needs and a greater say in the kind of care or assistance they receive.

- *Theme 3: the challenges of planning and organising care* – these involve not only setting up systems that respond to changing need and are accountable in appropriate ways but also designing places and spaces in which care can take place. There is growing recognition that users can play a part in all aspects of services – planning, service delivery, monitoring, as well as in the education of those who give care. Many groups in the voluntary sector have not only lobbied for change but have set up services to meet the needs of particular groups – for example, people with learning difficulties, women, minority ethnic groups. There may well be lessons to draw from this for the statutory sector.

I think of these themes as a K100 ABC:

---

**K100 ABC**

A    Acknowledging the complexity of the concept of care and its devaluation.

B    Building a better understanding of care relationships and care needs from the insights from research and user accounts.

C    Creating more responsive structures to provide a positive experience both for users of care services and for providers of those services.

---

Activity 7    **Using the K100 ABC**

Allow about 20 minutes

Write the themes of the K100 ABC at the top of three sheets of paper. List the seven blocks under each. Then see what you can jot down from the block material as relevant to each heading. You won't be able to find something for each theme from every block, but see how far you get.

You might want to have just a quick try at this activity now and do it properly at a later stage of your revision.

Comment

No two answers to this activity will be identical and one person's jottings will probably not make a lot of sense to anyone else. However, below we have put together some suggestions to help you make connections of your own between the blocks. But don't worry if your own answers are much more sketchy and take a different line. The important thing is to keep thinking through the course material in different ways – and so become more and more familiar with it. Remember that what follows is just one person's reading of how the course hangs together. By agreeing or disagreeing you will be beginning to construct your own.

If the K100 ABC does not appeal to you as a way of bringing things together, we suggest two other possibilities at the end of the section.

---

**A    Acknowledging the complexity of the concept of care and its devaluation**

(Blocks 1, 2, 3, 7; also 4 and 5)

Unit 1 defined an informal carer as someone who 'does some tasks for someone (or some people) who are unable to do them for themselves'. It focused on unpaid care in the home. It emphasised that this 'informal care' consists of more than simply carrying out tasks for another person. Informal caring is done 'for love', or out of a sense of duty or moral obligation, and conflicting emotions on both sides of the caring relationship can influence how it is seen and whether it is experienced by both parties as a burden or a blessing. Questions of how to handle reciprocity, power and dependency in the caring relationship emerge from the research. A central theme of the unit was that *associating caring with women's 'natural' work in the home has devalued it; so that these complex demands of caring and the skills needed for it are rarely brought out into the open for discussion.*

---

Devaluation of care affects paid carers too. Unit 3 showed how the skills of home carers (also mostly women) went unrecognised – a point picked up again in Block 7 (Unit 26) which discussed the uneven development of vocational qualifications and continuing low pay. Unit 2 showed how care can be difficult to define for hospital nurses and for health care assistants. It can slip down the agenda when the main focus is on the cure activities of doctors and when routines can take priority over just being with someone. In residential settings shortages of time and lack of training and support for staff can mean that care degenerates into rapid and inhumane processing of people. The case of Cedar Court was discussed in Unit 4, in Unit 8, and again in Unit 18. Some of the consequences of assuming that anyone can do a caring job and that training is unnecessary became very apparent in the fictional case of Marie at the beginning of Unit 18. Concepts such as 'intimate care' and 'emotional labour' are helping to clarify the demands of caring and are beginning to be used in training materials for paid carers of different kinds. More is being done also to support informal carers – the Carers (Recognition and Services) Act (Unit 1) is one sign of this, though Bibbings in the Course Reader argues that getting support is still a lottery and not enough is being done.

Just as care needs to be discussed more widely and understood better, so the assumptions about who is available to do it need to be put under the spotlight. The 'caring family' may not be in a position to offer care, especially with changes in women's employment and trends in household composition (Units 1, 6). Devaluation of care is a theme here too, insofar as it is still often assumed that caring can be treated as a family affair or something that will be undertaken by friends and neighbours. Much caring remains hidden in the 'private' area of the 'home' as discussed in Unit 6.

Spending time trying to define care and uncover the different dimensions of it is not just an academic exercise. How we think about care as a society will determine what resources are devoted to it. It will profoundly shape the experiences of those who are dependent on others for the quality of their daily lives.

## B Building a better understanding of care relationships and care needs

(Blocks 1, 2, 4, 5, 7; also 3 and 6)

Even well-meaning caregivers can get it wrong. Val Hollingshurst (Unit 1) learnt an important lesson from what she at first thought was a mistake of closing the thermos flask too tightly. Esther, whom you heard on Audio Cassette 2, struggled to stop her home carers from taking over things she felt she could do and wanted to do. The K100 principles of good practice (Unit 5) – enabling people to develop their own potential and have a voice, respecting their beliefs and preferences, promoting and supporting their rights to appropriate services, respecting their privacy and rights to confidentiality – all these can go some way to remedying such problems. But things are not always easy. There are instances where care workers need to weigh these values against other considerations and override them (social workers, for example, may decide that child protection overrides a parent's wishes, and care staff – in the day centre for Mr Bright in Unit 7 or in a residential home like Liberty of Earley House in

Unit 8 – may decide that because risks are too great, respect for preferences must be curtailed). The need to achieve a balance on confidentiality is discussed at length in Unit 23. The question of how to treat someone as a whole person, how to respect and sometimes help to rebuild their identity, as in reminiscence work, was examined in Unit 14.

Unit 4 showed how care relationships are always a matter of definitions which are negotiated from both sides, some aspects being particularly sensitive because they involve intimate care, touch and respect. Privacy and its importance was a key theme of Unit 7. How care is experienced depends very much on how relationships are defined. You saw in Unit 20 how vulnerable a new mother was to the definitions of care relationships projected by care workers from different services. Modelling care relationships on friendship has problems (Unit 3, Unit 26) but so too does modelling them on expertise. Some have questioned just how relevant the biomedical model of care – with its assumption of the doctor as professional expert and the patient as passive and dependent and taking on the 'sick role' (Unit 14) – is in health and social care situations today. Readings in Unit 2 challenged this for chronic ill health (Pinder) and for childbirth (Doyal). Chapter 19 by Jenny Morris strongly repudiated care that made physically disabled women more dependent. She advocates replacing a 'care model' with a 'rights model' where it would be possible to employ personal assistants directly and have more control over the work that they did (see Unit 3). Government documents have referred to patients and clients as 'consumers' who are entitled to greater choice than they have had in the past. Units 3, 10 and 27 discuss the limits of this, and Baldock and Ungerson's research (Reader Chapter 29) offers a caution. Yet there are signs of a more active consumerism (Unit 22, see also Unit 2, Unit 27). Paul Theobold (Unit 14, Audio Cassette 4), talking of how self-help groups and organisations have grown up, how he became expert in AIDS and was able to help others with his condition, might be an example of this.

When a group of people needing care is gathered under the same roof they run the risk of experiencing the depersonalised care regime associated with the concept of institutionalisation. That emerged vividly from the Lennox Castle video used in Block 4. The history of long-stay closed institutions is covered in Unit 16, though the account is careful to consider the quality of the evidence and weigh up good as well as bad. Institutional care comes up again in the context of abuse in Block 5 where Wardaugh and Wilding's model of how the 'corruption of care' occurs is given prominence. Much is made in Block 2 of the Wagner Report on residential care and Unit 8 is largely given over to the question of whether all residential care must necessarily become institutional. Unit 15 uses the work of Duffy and McCarthy to show how responsibility can be handed over to residents, in this case teenage girls. This case demonstrates how the staff needed support in changing their roles and facilitating the young women and enabling them to take responsibility. The discussion of a need for a 'new professionalism' in Unit 26 is relevant to this.

Duffy and McCarthy's work with groups rather than one-to-one with individuals is echoed in Block 3. The diversity of the population, the variability in resources available to people in very different circumstances, as well as differences in their history and cultural values, demand a more differentiated response. The ways in which racism has and has not been acknowledged emerge at a number of points, for example in Unit 8, in relation to needs of black groups for residential care, in Unit 27 concerning legacies from the welfare state in the 1940s, but most particularly through the powerful case material in Unit 11. Meanwhile, as Unit 12 shows, it is vital to recognise the special needs of communities where accumulated disadvantages have created conditions of social exclusion, which impact particularly powerfully on older people and on the formative experiences and life chances of children and young people.

## C   Creating more responsive structures ...

(Blocks 2, 3, 6, 7; also 4 and 5)

Again and again in the course, there have been examples of how care services – often quite unintentionally – fail to serve the needs of all of those for whom they were designed. The Black and minority ethnic groups in Unit 11 provide one example of pressing for change in statutory services which seem to have neglected particular needs or failed to understand specific circumstances and organising to provide alternatives. The proposals of the Black Perspectives Sub-Group on residential care, as set out in the Reader (Chapter 11), are relevant again here. Sometimes what is needed is a change to structures or procedures. Sometimes it is a matter of physical design – the layout of an antenatal waiting area, for example, and the facilities it offers (Unit 6) or the provision of adaptations to kitchens and bathrooms, small things that can make a world of difference to a person like Esther Hurdle from Unit 6, whom you heard on Audio Cassette 2. Sometimes, where unco-ordinated, piecemeal efforts at support have failed, it is a matter of a coherent, planned upgrading of the physical, social and economic environment, to overcome social exclusion, or there is a need for a national initiative such as Sure Start to give a new impetus to addressing long-standing needs (Unit 12). Sometimes, however, it is a matter of a fundamentally different way of thinking about what care aims to achieve (Morris is again an example). Self-help groups (Unit 14) often seek changes in the goals of services as well as facilitating self-expression and confidence via groupwork (Unit 15). The self-advocacy movement (Unit 22) sometimes goes further to confront and challenge service providers. In K100, it certainly becomes clear that it is not enough to 'treat everyone the same' and assume that all can access services equally (see especially Units 10 and 11).

The changes of the 1990 NHS and Community Care Act brought a belief that greater choice would occur through the implementation of the market principles of the New Right (Unit 27). The model of service user as a 'consumer' brought charters promising particular levels of service and, through publication of community care plans and plans for purchasing health services in a locality, the opportunity of greater public involvement in decisions about services in a locality (Unit 22). But just as service users are not fully involved as partners at the level of their own care, nor can we say yet that they are participating fully in planning and monitoring services. Unit 27 picks up this theme again and discusses a ladder of involvement where few have reached the top rung. But it also points to a policy world that has been transformed since the days of Beveridge. Services, and also professions, are becoming more accountable (Unit 24, Unit 26). Many more voices are making themselves heard in policy debates about care, however imperfect the structures for responding still are.

Change is perhaps the most appropriate note to end on – change in society and change in care services. Taking the long historical view, you could argue that society's thinking about care has been transformed.

- Labels like 'mental defectives', 'lunatics', 'the subnormal' and 'cripples' have been rejected.

- The long-stay institutions with their harsh regimes have been closed.

- We are prepared, in a way that was unthinkable even 20 years ago, to accept the possibility that there has been physical and sexual abuse of children and vulnerable adults, and to try to do something about this through policy development and inspection and monitoring.

- The silence about the extent to which many women's lives are dominated by the need to care for others has been replaced by the naming of people as 'carers' and by a concern to find ways to support them in the care that they do.

- Issues of racism in service functioning and service delivery are being acknowledged and combated through a wide array of policies and projects.

- Voluntary groups, self-help groups and advocacy groups have flourished to make the needs of client groups known as never before.

- We are a better informed and less deferential society, and have much higher expectations than previous generations regarding information about and involvement in shaping health and social care.

But all this, you will rightly say, is too positive. Institutional care remains even though the long-stay institutions have gone. We are not yet effectively preventing abuse – new scandals emerge with what seems to be increasing frequency. Carers are still campaigning and no doubt there are still many locked into care relationships that bring no pleasure to either party. Poverty, unemployment, disadvantage and lack of resources of all kinds, as well as pain and fear, make many people acutely vulnerable when faced with care services, and unable to act in partnership and to feel empowered. In short, as society changes, so do ideas about care – but not enough, and not backed by sufficient resources and political will. There is still much to debate and much to change.

I wonder how you reacted to that particular 'helicopter' view of the course? You might be saying to yourself, 'I couldn't have done that, but now I come to read it, yes, it is helpful in bringing it together.' But perhaps you think in different ways and it leaves you cold. I promised you two alternatives. As a first alternative, you could read through the section introductions in the Course Reader. Together they offer another 'helicopter' view that covers a great deal of the course material. You will be surprised how much sense they make to you now you have read most of the book.

I asked Andy Northedge for another way of pulling materials together. His answer is shown in the box below. It does not try to find overarching themes and to explain what has been going on in the world of care in the same way, but instead concentrates on four areas that the course material has covered – the many *settings* in which care takes place, the question of achieving high *standards* in giving care, the *structures* that have been created to enable care to happen, and care in relation to our *selves*, its meaning in our daily lives. Looked at in this way, there is definite overlap, but the emphasis is rather different.

---

**K100 and the four 'S's**

**Settings**

*Domestic homes*

– sites of informal and formal care (Blocks 1 and 2)

*Residential and hospital care*

– the physical environment (Block 2)

– regimes (Blocks 2 and 4)

– relationships within groups (Block 4)

*Communities*

– accessibility, diversity, change (Blocks 3 and 1)

**Standards**

Values and principles of good practice (all the skills units, and throughout the course)

Bad practice, lapses, codes of practice (Block 5)

Accountability, record keeping (Block 6)

**Structures**

Vocations, professions – training, careers (Block 7)

State provided services vs. the market model (Blocks 7 and 1)

Legislation, policies (Care Systems and Structures)

**Selves**

Carers' and care receivers' lives, personal histories, identities (Block 4)

---

ABC, four 'S's or something of your own – all of these are ways of revisiting the material, capturing bits of it in a particular net, seeing some of the connections, and generally helping to make it stick. Use what is useful, discard what is not.

One aim of the course team in producing K100 was to draw many different people into the debate about 'who cares?'. Almost three thousand students registered for K100 in its first year. In a decade's time, then, there may be approaching thirty thousand more informed people asking questions about care, taking part perhaps in projects for change and insisting that their experience and their needs be heard. It is quite a thought.

*Taking a 'helicopter view' of the course*

# Section 4
# Conclusion

The aim of this unit has been to help you see K100 as a whole and to make connections between its elements. The revision activities, the quizzes, the extended discussion of the K100 ABC, have all been different means to this end. But K100 is not like a jigsaw – there is no one way in which all the elements fit together to a form a picture that is perfect and complete. The links that you make, the elements that stick in your mind, will reflect your own personal history and interests. What you make of it will never be quite the same as what someone else does. It is a resource – perhaps a resource that you will continue to use in your life even when the exam is over.

In the Introduction and Study Guide we set out the aims of the course in the following words.

> *The course aims to:*
> * *contribute to improved practice in health and social care*
> * *enhance knowledge and understanding of health and social care across a wide range of settings and situations*
> * *encourage constructive reflection on personal experience of care relationships*
> * *supply the knowledge base for progress to professionally recognised qualifications in health and social care*
> * *provide a learning framework which will equip students with the study skills necessary to succeed at degree level study.*

If you have worked steadily through the course during the year – if you have carried out most of the activities, read the readings, completed the TMAs and finally worked your way through this revision unit – you have achieved these aims. Once the exam is successfully out of the way, you will also have 60 points of credit towards a degree and be eligible for a Certificate in Health and Social Care.

Good luck in the exam and I hope you will want to study further courses in the field of health and social welfare with The Open University.

# Section 5
# Appendix: Help with the quizzes

## Quick Quiz 1:
## 'Top ten' readings from K100

There is no 'right' answer to this, but here is my own response. It draws on Reader chapters only. Your answer might include some of the offprints too.

I'd start with **Morris** (Reader Chapter 19). This gives you such a vivid sense of what it feels like to be on the receiving end of care and raises so many questions about dependence and independence, as well as giving you an insight into how care came onto the public agenda, and how ways of seeing are also ways of not seeing, and how we need to enlarge our visions of care. Then, but perhaps it is cheating, because it has so many users' voices in it, I would want to include the anthology chapter by **Bornat** (Chapter 1). Care settings and care policies have changed but there are still many echoes of what some of those people describe. Next I think of **Lawler** (Chapter 26), who puts into words what intimate care entails, raises questions of touch and taboo and of emotional involvement, which are all part and parcel of what caring is but are often just ignored. Next, I'd pull together a clutch of things – **Jones and Fowles's** summary of Goffman's thinking on total institutions (Chapter 8), **Lee Treweek's** study of Cedar Court (Chapter 25), and **Wardaugh and Wilding** (Chapter 24) who summarise, synthesise and develop a model of how and why the 'corruption of care' can occur. **Shah** (Chapter 21) has to be on my list as a reminder of all the issues around acknowledging diversity and developing care services that can respond. **Baldock and Ungerson's** (Chapter 29) stroke sufferers dealing with the mixed economy of care come up in Unit 10, and again in Unit 27. They are an important reminder of how vulnerable people cannot always be the active consumers that government policy documents sometimes assume. **Twigg** (Chapter 30), asking important questions about the line between health and social care, gives another important perspective on how policy is affecting people in ways we might not want to support. I would like **Annandale** (Chapter 31) on the list to remind me of the strains on workers of providing care and of how 'defensive practice' needs to be understood before it can be changed (although perhaps I might just choose **Heller** (Chapter 5) to do this instead).

## Quick Quiz 2:
## Who wrote what?

You will find the eight authors in the following blocks (some authors appear in other blocks too):

1    Wallcraft – Block 6

2    Shah – Block 3

3    Doyal – Block 1

4    Duffy and McCarthy – Block 4

5    Williams – Block 7

6    Killick – Block 4

7    Dartington Social Research Unit – Block 5

8    Willcocks, Peace and Kelleher – Block 2

## Quick Quiz 3:
## Who is or was...?

You will find the people mentioned here in the following blocks:

Henry Mayhew – Block 4

Lady Rhys-Williams – Block 7

Erving Goffman – Block 1

Lady Gillian Wagner – Block 2

John Bowlby – Block 1

Peter Townsend – Blocks 1 and 4

Erik Erikson – Block 4

William Beveridge – Block 7

## Quick Quiz 4:
## What is meant by...?

You will find these concepts mentioned in the following blocks (some concepts appear in other blocks too):

Defensive practice – Block 6

Emotional labour – Block 1

Vulnerable adults – Block 5

Scripts – Block 1

Active consumerism – Block 6

Private space – Block 2

Stereotyping – Block 3

Identity – Block 4

Informal carers – Block 1

Institutional racism – Block 3

Self-advocacy – Block 6

Self-help groups – Block 4

Sick role – Block 4

Social exclusion – Block 3

Disabling environments – Block 2

Eugenics – Block 4

New professionalism – Block 7

Institutionalisation – Block 2

Community action – Block 3

Social Darwinism – Block 4

The New Right – Block 7

New managerialism – Block 6

Behavioural programmes – Block 5

Normalisation – Block 2

# Section 6
# Linking K100 studies to professional training

**Healthcare connections**

This block looks at how policy affects the provision of healthcare and ways of working.

**Qualifications and training**

Statistics show huge numbers working in healthcare classified as professionals, associate professionals and health related, yet they still do not include everyone employed in healthcare.

Qualifications for this immense workforce are, for historical reasons, divided into (i) VQs acquired 'on the job' by nursing auxiliaries like Lucy and care assistants working in care homes such as Lathbury Manor and (ii) more academically taught professional qualifications. VQs enable skills to be recognised, giving workers confidence, and helping raise standards of care in areas where training has long been neglected. VQs are developed to map on to current practice within frameworks set to national standards. By contrast, health professions regulate their own qualifications, according to their own values and standards. However, under criticism, the professions are becoming more outward looking, open and accountable and inter-professional flexibility and responsiveness are being encouraged.

**State services versus the market**

Public support for the NHS has remained high since Beveridge's plan to attack the 'five giants' was implemented by the post-war Labour government. However, structures and organisation of the NHS have changed over the years (e.g. the original tripartite structure). Reorganisation of general practice has led to current policies favouring a more integrated service with a focus on primary care.

The New Right criticised what were seen as inefficiencies, inadequacies and excessive costs, introducing market thinking and discouraging dependency on the state. New Labour has shifted the emphasis to 'modernisation', management and standard setting, with a plethora of new initiatives. Consequently, in recent times, healthcare workers have found their roles and practices under continual review and open to much public debate and criticism, creating much uncertainty, while opening up new opportunities.

**User voices**

How well has the perspective of service users been represented within all this change? Unit 27 considers the role of user groups and user expectations in creating a flexible, responsive healthcare service.

**Study skills**

Unit 28 reviews the study skills you have developed throughout K100. Many of these skills, such as organisation and time management, are readily transferable to healthcare situations. Study skills also enable healthcare workers to embrace lifelong learning, keeping themselves up to date with fast moving changes in healthcare as new policies and technologies are introduced.

### Social work connections

### Social work as part of social care

It is important that social workers recognise that they are only a small part of the workforce that delivers social care. Although social work does not compare favourably to some occupations, within the social care workforce social workers enjoy a relatively privileged position in terms of status and salaries.

### Social work as a profession

Social work training places much emphasis on practising professionally and becoming a member of the social work profession. The debate about professionalism in social work, discussed in Unit 26, recognises that social work does not enjoy the status of the 'old' professions such as law or medicine. The introduction of a regulatory body, the *General Social Care Council*, together with the development of post-qualifying training, reflects an attempt to enhance the professionalisation of social work. The extending of social work training to a three-year degree was influenced both by the competency framework of NVQs and the more traditional academic models.

### The changing context of practice

Social work has developed against a backdrop of major change in social policy over the past 60 years. The post-war introduction of the welfare state and its subsequent evolution substantially shaped the institutions and practices of social work. Then over the past two decades the New Right policies of the Conservatives, subsequently modified and extended by New Labour, have led to further fundamental changes such as the development of a mixed economy of care and the repositioning of the role of the social worker within the policy of care in the community.

### Service user perspectives

Block 7 returns to a key theme in K100 and within social work: how to enable people to contribute to shaping the services they use. Unit 27 concludes optimistically that future services users may have a greater say. Social workers are uniquely placed to influence the debate as to how this can happen.

### Children and young people: connections

### The changing social context

Block 7 places work with children and young people within a broad context of sweeping change over the past half century. Even the cover picture speaks volumes. Income levels have risen; class structures have changed; people are more mobile; families have shrunk in size; patterns of family life have been transformed; many more mothers take paid work; child minding has become an established field of work with its own training and qualifications; children quickly become immersed in TV, the internet, computer games and consumer culture, while young people engage, or not, with a variety of vigorous youth sub-cultures. Education has gone through a series of transformations. New kinds of child experts have emerged. New names and descriptions of conditions have appeared, such as dyslexia, attention deficit syndrome and autism. Attitudes towards children, families, parenting, authority, discipline, religion and the meaning of life have changed, and British society has become more ethnically diverse, broadening the range of patterns of child-rearing. Against this backdrop, work with children and young people has, of course, changed enormously.

### The changing political context

As you read in Unit 27, a fundamental force for change was the post-war development of the Beveridge-inspired welfare state. Following the establishment of the NHS, children were checked, weighed and measured and given free milk, orange juice and cod-liver oil, as the state set out to take responsibility for the wellbeing and healthy development of all children. School-leaving ages were raised and grammar schools and secondary moderns introduced, later to be replaced by comprehensive schools. Eventually the New Right came to see this ambition to care for all children and young people as too expensive, too inflexible, too bureaucratic and too interfering on the part of a 'nanny state'. Instead parents were to be seen as 'consumers' on behalf of their children, making personally appropriate choices rather than accepting universal provision. Levels of funding for health and social care services and education were held down in the interests of achieving greater efficiency and value for money. Subsequently New Labour has increased funding levels, but has also set targets aimed at modernising state service provision. It has also targeted child poverty and social exclusion.

If we stand back from the detail and the ebb and flow of policy it remains clear that the establishment of universal education, health care and the child protection services in the last 50 years has transformed the lives of children and young people alive today.

### Changing occupational structures

In the context of all this change many new roles have emerged in work with children and young people. The table in Unit 26 shows the very large numbers employed specifically in work with children and young people, though most of the other occupations listed would include work with children and young people.

### Changing training and qualifications

Not only have new categories of work with children and young people been created, but there is a greater emphasis on training and qualifications. This includes practical work-based training leading to NVQs and more academically oriented professional training and qualifications (Unit 26).

### Changing professional boundaries

But as areas of specialist work with children and young people have multiplied and structures of service provision have become more complex and more diverse (particularly since the devolving of powers to Scotland, Wales and Northern Ireland) there has also been a growing recognition of the need to break down boundaries between professions and to develop ways of working in interdisciplinary teams (Unit 26, Section 5). This is particularly important in the case of work with children and young people because of their relative vulnerability.